HELPING ELDERLY PARENTS

HELPING ELDERLY PARENTS

The Role of Adult Children

VICTOR G. CICIRELLI
Purdue University

 Auburn House Publishing Company
Boston, Massachusetts

The work on which this volume is based was supported by grants from the Andrus Foundation of the National Retired Teachers Association and the American Association of Retired Persons, 1909 K Street, N.W., Washington, D.C.

Library of Congress Cataloging in Publication Data

Cicirelli, Victor G.
  Helping elderly parents.

  Includes index.
  1. Parents, Aged—United States—Family
  relationships. I. Title. II. Title: Adult children.
  HQ1064.U5C45   646.7′8   81-10880
  ISBN 0-86569-080-4   AACR2

Printed in the United States of America

FOREWORD

With the steady increase in both the number and proportion of elderly persons in the United States, attention must be given to the role of the family, particularly adult children, as providers of the primary support system for the elderly. The great majority of older persons are able to and do care for themselves. Regardless of age, they wish to remain independent as long as possible. For those who cannot do so, including some segments of the aging population which are increasing more rapidly, the elderly prefer assistance from their adult children. This is consonant with the traditional pattern of mutual aid between elderly parents and their adult children.

Traditional family life patterns and relationships, including intergenerational expectations and capacities, are being altered by major social, economic, and cultural changes. To understand these factors we need to know more about the nature of caring relationships between elderly parents and adult children. How do elderly parents and their adult children view the need for various kinds of services for the parents? Do parents and children agree on which services are important and who should provide them? Is there a potential conflict between elderly parents' needs for help from their children and the amount of help that the children are willing and able to provide? What kinds of help are provided by adult children? What psycho-social variables sustain or hinder the helping behavior of adult children toward elderly dependent parents over long periods of time? How do elderly parents and their adult children feel about services provided by others?

These and other related issues are examined carefully by Victor G. Cicirelli. This volume is based on his recent field studies on the role of adult children in helping elderly parents and draws on his previous research on the human life cycle. His findings confirm other research for discarding the "myth of abandonment," but he cautions against the dangers of embracing the other extreme of total commitment.

A few years ago, the editors of *Daedalus* noted there was no substantial scholarly literature on the subject of generations. The findings and resulting recommendations of this study have theoretical and practical implications for gerontologists, service providers, counselors, and researchers and for development of public social policy. The subject is illuminated when placed within a life span perspective that views parent care as part of an intergenerational life span sequence.

While national programs such as Social Security and Medicare provide basic benefits, other services may be needed to enable the elderly to live independent and fuller lives. These include homemaking, transportation, maintenance, home health care, bureaucratic mediation, and protection. These are provided by the family, voluntary organizations and agencies, governmental agencies, neighbors, and friends. Such services are rendered by the family and formal providers, but they must be coordinated and monitored. Adult children can do this more effectively when assisted by adequate incentives and support programs, and the author presents practical suggestions to this end.

The author recognizes that the interaction between adult children and elderly parents in the process of helping is not a simple matter, and he offers thoughtful recommendations. To paraphrase Goethe—to grow old is in itself to enter upon a new venture. This book will aid the partners in this venture, elderly dependent parents and their adult children, as well as professionals and other care providers.

FREDERICK J. FERRIS
NRTA-AARP Andrus Foundation

PREFACE

This book represents the culmination of two studies sponsored by the NRTA-AARP Andrus Foundation. The first study was primarily concerned with determining the elderly's needs and desires for various services in relation to the kin network. A major finding was that the elderly, regardless of age, wanted to remain independent for as long as possible, but if help was needed they wished it to come from their children. This finding, confirmed by findings of others, stimulated the formulation of the second study. We were interested in looking at the other side of the coin to see how adult children felt about providing help to parents. Was there a potential conflict between elderly parents' desire for help from children and the amount of help which the children were capable and willing to provide? Did parents and children agree on which services were important, or was there a mismatch?

The notion that adult children neglect their parents has been labeled the "myth of abandonment," but the opposite notion, that adult children have sufficient commitment to provide effective help, may be emerging as a new myth. If there are limitations to adult children's helping behaviors, then it is important to clarify the extent of their role as helpers and to determine the psychological characteristics which influence their helping behaviors. Through such an understanding it may be possible to modify and sustain adult children's helping behavior in the face of the many obstacles in modern society.

One theme developed in the book is that adult children are not only the primary helpers of elderly parents, but can best serve as the coordinators of other providers when their parents become more dependent. A second theme, which could have longer-range effects, is the promotion of the elderly's capability of and willingness for self-help. The ideal is to encourage life styles that will allow people to continue personal growth until almost the very end of life.

I am deeply grateful to the Andrus Foundation of the NRTA-AARP for its continued and generous support of my work. Particular thanks are due to Dr. Frederick J. Ferris, Mary Louise Luna, and the Board of the Andrus Foundation, for their interest and encouragement of my studies.

I also wish to express my appreciation to the elderly members of the Lafayette community, to the adult children of the elderly who shared their views with us, and to the many individuals from community agencies and organizations who gave us advice and information about the elderly in the Lafayette community.

Finally, I would like to acknowledge the contribution of my conscientious and hard-working research assistants who carried out the interviewing in the field for the two studies: Ruth Chaffee, Barbara Chattin-McNichols, David Conners, Gloria Cox, Charlotte Crucean, Deborah Doss, Virginia Hoegler, Tara Lavelle, Barbara Mosbacher, Jon Nussbaum, Christa Pena, Maura Stilson, and Philip Sutton.

V.G.C.

CONTENTS

LIST OF TABLES

HELPING ELDERLY PARENTS

Part One

SIGNIFICANCE OF ADULT CHILDREN TO THEIR ELDERLY PARENTS

Chapter 1

ADULT CHILDREN AS SERVICE PROVIDERS

Elderly Americans are remaining vigorous longer than ever before. However, those segments of the elderly population that are increasing most rapidly—women over 65 years of age and the "old-old" (both men and women over age 75)—include many people with chronic conditions. These elderly people have the greatest need for help. Careful planning of services for these elderly, directly, indirectly through others, or through self-help programs, is important if their needs are to be met.

Many elderly are able to care for their own needs until late in life, and little, if any, essential help is needed from their adult children, other kin, or other nonfamily support systems.[1-3] The desire of the elderly to be self-sufficient and provide for their own needs suggests the importance of intervention programs to help them to maintain their independence as long as possible.[4,5]

However, almost everyone, except those who die abruptly, eventually goes through a period of decline and increasing dependency when some outside help is needed, and the family has usually provided at least part of this help.

In 1978 and early 1979, a survey was conducted[1] among elderly residents of a small midwestern city of approximately 60,000 people to determine the kinds of services they used and desired, who provided such services, and who they desired to provide services if they were not able to care for themselves in the future.

One major finding of the study was that although most of the elderly interviewed took care of their own needs, at a future time when they could no longer provide for themselves they would prefer

3

their adult children to help them rather than other kin or nonfamily support systems. For example, governmental help was desired only through such well-established programs as housing, Medicare, Medicaid, and Social Security.

Traditionally, elderly parents were cared for by their adult children and other family members, and public help was not involved until the adult children had done all they could. Today, adult children still help their elderly parents and make it possible for them to stay out of institutions, remaining in their own homes or living with their adult children. Adult children are essential as service providers to help satisfy the needs of elderly parents.

Evidence for the Family as a Support System

Research over the past two decades led to the conclusion that most elderly are not abandoned, neglected, isolated, or rejected by their adult children or other kin. Most elderly live near at least one adult child, with whom they have frequent contact and exchange of services.[6-11] As elderly people grow still older, lose friends, and become more dependent, they become more involved with their families than with nonkin.[12] Ties with family members may be the only remaining attachments they have,[13] and adult children become more important for assistance.[14-16]

There is a pattern of mutual aid between adult children and their elderly parents which continues for as long as the parents are able. In some cases, particularly at higher socioeconomic levels, elderly parents, almost to the ends of their lives, continue to provide more help to adult children than their children do to them. However, when parents attain advanced old age, with concomitant mental and physical deterioration—loss of vigor, decline in health, and possibly a disability or handicap—widowhood, loss of income after retirement, or a combination of these factors, the balance shifts, and adult children provide greater amounts of aid to elderly parents. In fact, adult children (the middle generation) tend to give more help to both the older and younger generations than they receive from either.[13, 17]

This approach seems justified in view of studies[19, 20] which found children provide help to their elderly parents or influence the affection and emotional satisfaction of both giver and receiver,[18] the primary concern of this study is with the adult children's provision of services to their elderly parents, regardless of any reciprocation by the parents.

This approach seems justified in view of studies[19, 20] which found that the flow of services to a dependent parent was different in kind from those services which were mutually exchanged between elderly parents who were independent and their married children. Also, when help was needed, adult children clearly gave more help than they received.[21]

The type of help provided seems to vary with families, their circumstances, and their previous history of helping each other. One type of help which most families provide is help in a crisis situation. Sussman[12] reports that in a crisis situation which is the result of accident, illness, or other emergency, the kin members are quick to give aid to the elderly person. The adult children tend to bear the main burden. The amount of assistance and the length of time it is offered depend on the already-established family helping patterns. If the elderly parents had been isolated, they are more likely to be given only minimal aid to get through the emergency period. After this, conditions return to the status quo. Bild and Havighurst[6] found that 88% to 98% of their seven subsamples of elderly had someone who could be relied upon in an emergency, and from 68% to 95% had someone who could come in to give care in time of illness. Thus, overall, for the great majority of elderly, the kin network is a viable source of contact and mutual aid. Children are regarded as the closest kin for the elderly, with siblings next in order of importance.

According to Shanas,[10] the spouse and children of the old person are the major support in time of illness, based on a 1975 national survey of noninstitutionalized elderly. In an earlier study, Shanas *et al.*[11] found that in Denmark, Britain, and the United States there were more bedfast older persons at home than in all types of institutions; these elderly were being cared for by their families, who provided the necessary supporting services to prevent institutionalization. In most cases, this was accomplished without help of formal community services. Shanas[22] reported that in time of illness, one-third to two-fifths of the elderly rely on spouses and a similar proportion relies on adult children and other kin. Among those who were considered bedfast at home, 80% to 90% depended on family members for meals, housework, personal help, and so on. Thus it seems that adult children provide much help in illness or crisis situations, and numerous studies attest to the importance and reliability of this kind of help from children.

However, adult children help their parents in many areas other than care in illness. In a study carried out by Shanas,[23] seven of every ten elderly persons reported that they receive some kind of help from their children. In addition to care in illness, this help included home repairs, housework, negotiations with bureaucracy, and various gifts. Bracey[24] found that the most frequent services received by elderly parents from adult children were shopping, housework, cooking, and advisory help about financial and maintenance matters. However, Bracey found that less than 15% of the elderly received regular help; regular financial help was received by no more than 9%.

Housework and shopping seem to be areas in which adult children typically provide services to elderly parents, along with house maintenance and repairs. Protection and negotiation with the bureaucracy are types of services that are highly important in today's world. Financial assistance and gifts do not seem to be as important as other forms of help.

Sussman and Burchinal[25] suggested that emotional support by adult children has replaced the actual physical support for the elderly. This, of course, reflects the increase in services provided for the elderly by nonfamily providers. While it is questionable that children's physical help to elderly parents has been replaced, certainly their advisory roles and psychological support are becoming more important.

While the studies presented thus far do not constitute a complete review of the evidence for the family as a support system, they do indicate the important role of the adult child in providing help to their elderly parents. However, the quality of the services provided by adult children, the frequency of the services provided, the effectiveness of such services in providing solutions to the parents' needs or problems, and the elderly parents' satisfaction with the help received from their adult children have not been clearly determined thus far.

Regardless of the effectiveness of help provided by adult children to elderly parents and parents' satisfaction with it, adult children may not have the resources and skills to give sufficient help to their elderly parents. Adult children may not be able to provide intermittent or continuous long-term care of those elderly parents who have become quite dependent. The amount of help required may be so great a burden that the childrens' normal family functioning and morale are affected. On the other hand, those elderly parents who want to continue their personal growth and self-fulfillment but who need considerable family support to maintain their activities may also place a severe strain on adult children. Therefore, one should examine certain trends or factors that may limit the amount and kinds of help that adult children can provide.

Limitations of the Family Support System

Although industrialization and urbanization did not eliminate the extended family and its support system for the elderly, there are various demographic, social, and economic trends occurring today that may limit how much adult children are capable and willing to do to help their elderly parents.

Demographic Trends

During this century, there has been a steady increase in the number and proportion of individuals over age 65 in the United States. In 1900, there were approximately 3,000,000 people over age 65, who made up approximately 4% of the total population. In 1980, the number and proportion of elderly was projected to be approximately 24,000,000 and approximately 10% of the total population. By the year 2,000, the elderly will number approximately 29,000,000 and 11% of the total population.[26-28] By the year 2030, the number of elderly should reach 55,000,000—20% of the total population.

In addition, within the elderly group itself there has been a rapid increase in the number and proportion of the "old-old"—those individuals over age 75. In 1900, approximately 900,000, or 30% of the 3,000,000 elderly, were over age 75, but by 1980 there was projected to be approximately 9,000,000 of the old-old, making up 38% of the elderly population. By the year 2000, 12,000,000 old-old, or 40% of the elderly population, are projected. If the death rate for the elderly is lowered even slightly, as might occur with a reduction in the incidence of cancer or cardiorenal disease due to medical advances, still more elderly will live beyond age 75 and the proportion of the old-old will soar dramatically.[26]

Such changes in the elderly population have important implications. The advanced elderly and the group of elderly widows have special needs and require various special services if they are to continue to function at an adequate level. Adult children may not be able to care for so many diverse problems of the elderly. Secondly, they will have to deal with chronic conditions over much longer time periods as more elderly parents continue living to advanced old age. Third, as elderly live longer, there is an increased likelihood that adult children may need to provide help both for their own and for their spouses' parents for some period of time. Thus, the simple increase in numbers of elderly will place a greater burden on adult children.

Changes in the sex ratio of the elderly is another important trend. In addition to the fact that the elderly are increasing in number more rapidly than the general population with the proportion of advanced elderly increasing most of all, there has been an increase in both the number and proportion of elderly women compared to men. The exact reasons are not known, but it is suspected that men are more susceptible to stress, heart and respiratory diseases, and cancer.[29] In any event, women can expect to live approximately eight years longer than men at the present time. It is anticipated that this difference will increase in the years to come, implying that there will be more widows with all the concomitant problems of widowhood.[26, 30]

In 1930, the sex ratio for those over 65 years of age was 100; that is, for every 100 men aged 65 and over, there were 100 women. In 1977 the sex ratio was about 69, which means that there were far more elderly women than men.[31] As previously stated, elderly women are continuing to live longer than men. In previous decades, when one of the elderly parents became dependent, the spouse could take care of him or her, and they could thus maintain their independence as a couple for a longer period of time. However, with the change in sex ratio and the increasing number of elderly widows, the burden of care will be on the adult children.

The modern family is shrinking in size. Aging parents have raised fewer children, and the number of adult children available to provide services for the elderly will soon be relatively fewer than in previous time periods.

Many of today's elderly were married in the depression years, and because such hard times made it difficult to fulfill marital aspirations and child-rearing plans, there were more one- and two-child families, more childless marriages, and more unmarried adults than in other periods.[32] These aging parents should now be in their mid-sixties or early seventies, and in many cases are experiencing the limited services that a smaller number of adult children can provide.

Whether more recent declines in birth rate can be attributed to increasing use of birth control measures as a result of the "zero population growth" appeal, to the currently less-favorable economic outlook (lack of job opportunities, inflation), to the feminist movement, or to other factors is not presently clear. However, if present trends continue, it has been estimated[32] that zero population growth may be a reality within fifty years. This would result in a dramatic increase in the proportion of childless, one-child, and two-child families in the population compared to the present family size mixture. With a reduction in the proportion of young children in the population, the overall dependency ratio (ratio of number of dependents to number of people of working age in the population, where dependents include children, aged, disabled, and so on) might be slightly less than it is today in spite of the increased number of elderly people. But the proportion of aged dependents would rise to about 40% of the dependency group.[28] This would mean that a considerable shift of national resources would need to be made from support of children to support of the elderly. If the one- or two-child family becomes the modal family size, the burden of caring for aging parents may be quite high compared to sharing the "load" with three or four adult children. The aging parent with few adult children—or none—may have to depend on the kin, such as siblings, for help. However, if families continue to become smaller, there will also be fewer siblings available.

Children of parents of advanced age, who are themselves aging, are becoming more prevalent. The advanced elderly or "old-old" (those over 75 years of age) are increasing at a more rapid rate than any other segment of the population. Although many of them may be quite healthy, the old-old in general require greater aid than the "young-old" (60–75). However, many adult children of the advanced elderly will themselves be reaching the young-old stage with a concomitant decline in energy, finances, and health. They will be preoccupied with dealing with their own problems of retirement and postretirement adjustment, and will have less ability to help their elderly parents.[33] In effect, two generations of elderly may have to be helped by other family members, thus enormously increasing the burden for the extended family.

As elderly people live to more advanced ages, they have a greater chance of becoming grandparents, great-grandparents, or even great-great-grandparents. The three-generation family is extremely prevalent; the four-generation family is now quite common, and the five-generation family is definitely on the increase.

In the three-generation family, the adult children must provide help not only to aging parents but also to their own young children. The question becomes one of who should have priority in the allocation of resources: the young children? the adult children themselves? or the elderly parents? This becomes a greater problem if resources are limited; but it will be compounded further if adult children also have to consider their own grandparents and even possibly their great-grandparents in a five-generation family.

Increased mobility of the population is another trend which limits family help. Children and other family members are not always available to the elderly because they have moved away. Rural elderly are likely to be somewhat isolated from young adult children because the latter tend to move away in search of better jobs. In suburbia, the elderly themselves may be quite mobile—for example, retired in Florida—and they may not live very close to other kin. Such migration decreases the availability of the extended family for certain segments of the elderly population (for example, the lower middle class).

All these demographic changes or trends now exist, and should limit in some degree the capability and willingness of adult children to provide help to their elderly parents. The extent to which they actually result in such limitations needs confirmation by further empirical studies.

Social Trends

Changes in women's roles in recent decades have important implications. Cultural changes are taking place in which women are becoming liberated from family duties and desire careers for their own self-fulfillment. Traditionally, it has been the female members of the extended family, and especially the adult female children, who have provided most of the services to the elderly. However, today's adult females, more than half of whom are employed outside the home, are now less available for helping the elderly than in previous times.[31]

In modern society, great value is placed on freedom and independence. As a result, adult children are often unwilling to sacrifice their own needs (and sometimes the needs of their children) to help the elderly, and elderly parents are inhibited from requesting such assistance. Helping behavior may thus be regarded as more voluntary than obligatory, depending more on respect and love than on guilt and shame.[34]

Differences in life styles are also occurring. Although adult children may be available to help in crisis situations, it may be difficult for them to be with their elderly parents on an extended or daily basis if the generations differ regarding values, interests, and general life style. For example, being together may create problems in terms of such simple preferences as liking different foods, liking different TV programs, going to bed and awakening at different times, having different approaches to housework, and so on.

Petrowsky[35] found high morale of elderly to be more strongly associated with interaction with friends and neighbors than with their adult children. He felt that one reason for this was the difference in such aspects of life style as values, hobbies, interests, attitudes and beliefs. Adult children and their parents may have little in common other than family, and thus may not make good companions. If this is true, there may be less commitment on the part of today's adult children to provide help to elderly parents, especially if any great sacrifices are involved.

Also, the elderly have a great need to deal with such problems as preventing social isolation, finding ways to use their time, and finding meaningful roles and status in the community. These are difficult needs to satisfy, and adult children do not seem best equipped to satisfy these needs for the elderly on a long-range basis.[36]

The emergence of new and variant family forms is another trend that may have an impact upon the elderly. Today, there is a great deal of diversity in family forms, and such variant family forms are increasingly found among middle-aged adult children. Although severely divergent forms, such as communes, group living, polygamy, and gay marriages, exist in relatively small numbers in the United States, they do represent a way of life that may have long-range implications for helping the elderly. Perhaps more important, because of the large numbers of people involved, is the increasing frequency of divorced, separated, widowed, and remarried middle-aged adult children. For one person to have a series of divorces and remarriages is also becoming more common in our culture. This form of marriage has been termed "serial monogamy."[37]

In all these cases, there is the possibility that family relationships will become blurred or be maintained with less sense of obligation. There might be less commitment and fewer resources to help elderly parents when adult children are involved in problems surrounding a divorce, or are adjusting to a remarriage. Where there have been several marriages, new spouses may pull the adult children away from elderly parents. The spouses are then likely to have little feeling of commitment to in-laws, especially if these are their second or even third set of in-laws. And, finally, adult children who are participating in less socially acceptable relationships—such as gay marriages—may be alientated from their elderly parents and feel unwilling to provide for them to any great extent.

Economic Trends

Inflation, with lessened purchasing power and increased cost of living, has been eroding the economic resources of the elderly and their adult children, simultaneously making the elderly more likely to need economic help and their adult children less able to provide it. A secondary effect has been the construction of smaller houses and small cars, both of which make it more difficult to provide elderly parents with housing and transportation. Also, not only do women leave the home to fulfill their career needs, but increasing numbers of married women work to provide an adequate family income in today's inflationary world. A two-worker income is becoming essential to maintaining the family's standard of living, which means that women are less available to help elderly parents. Finally, as the recession continues and jobs are lost, some middle-aged families migrate in search of jobs, increasing the geographical distance from their elderly parents and making it more difficult to be available for help.

Evidence exists to support each of the demographic, social, and economic trends which have been discussed thus far. It seems only logical that these trends will place some limitations on the family as a support system to the elderly, although future empirical studies are needed to bear this out. In the meantime, if adult children (and other family members) cannot satisfy all the needs of their elderly parents, then it becomes important to coordinate the family with other support systems to the elderly, recognizing their limitations also.

Limitations of Other Support Systems

Formal support systems (government agencies and voluntary organizations) are the first to be considered. Local, state, and federal government has had a relatively long history of providing help to the elderly. In fact, the government has had an expanding role with the advent of public housing, public health services (Medicare, Medicaid, Social Security), public transportation, and so on. The advantage of formal agencies is that they can provide services on a large scale to elderly throughout the country. For example, only the government has the resources to provide a health service such as Medicare.

However, there are also limitations. As Quinn and Hughston[38] have indicated, there is a continual shortage of professional and paraprofessional personnel trained to work with the elderly, and inflation is causing ever-rising costs of building formal support networks, training and hiring staff, and providing hospitalization.

Also, many elderly do not want to accept services from such agencies; it is embarrassing to them as they associate such services with being on welfare. Other elderly do not like the feeling of being dependent on someone else, especially some impersonal organization outside the family. Then, too, there may be the problem of dealing with a tremendous amount of "red tape" to determine eligibility and arrange for services. This inhibits many elderly from trying to obtain government services.

According to Quinn and Hughston,[38] the three most frequent criticisms of these formal groups are that they are: (1) inaccessible because of physical location or limited hours of service, (2) impersonal because they are uncaring in their treatment of persons in need of services, (3) inefficient because of their devotion to rules and procedures that interfere with service delivery. There is also the problem of quality and commitment of personnel in many formal agencies. (The conditions in nursing homes have been a national scandal in recent years.)

Finally, for the government to provide services of increasing quality and quantity for a growing population of elderly implies a continuous expansion of the economy. With the present slow rate of economic growth combined with inflation, the United States may not be in a position to provide more services in the near future. Also, the scarcity of qualified personnel, the low salaries and high turnover, and the lack of adequate training programs make it difficult to guarantee a high-quality program.

Voluntary agencies (Red Cross, Salvation Army, Family Service, Community Chest, church-related programs, and so on) are many and diverse, and have contributed in various ways to providing for the elderly, but as formal agencies, they, too, have many of the same limitations outlined above.

Hired help is considered to be a desirable service provider by many elderly and their families. Middle-class elderly can hire others to provide services more easily than lower-class elderly. When it can be done, it gives the elderly a greater sense of independence. By purchasing the service, they can continue to feel in charge of their own destiny. However, the majority of elderly are relatively poor or have limited incomes, and with today's inflation there are definite limitations on the amount of service the elderly can hire or purchase from others. Also, trustworthy, hardworking, and conscientious hired helpers for the elderly are difficult to find and retain.

Informal peer networks are another source of help. Neighbors, because they live close by, are well suited to provide immediate assistance and regular checkups on the well-being of the elderly. However, friends also provide such services.[39] According to Hess[40] and Rosow,[8] friends are important sources of emotional support, information, and opportunities for role rehearsal. Even one intimate friend may be sufficient in this regard.[41] Age-segregated living arrangements may help to provide suitable peers for interaction, and networks of mutual assistance may be developed.[8, 42, 43]

On the other hand, there are limitations here too. Mutual assistance and a sense of community do not necessarily result from contacts with neighbors and/or friends.[42] Lopata[44] noted that many of the widows she studied no longer made social contacts with neighbors. This may be a greater problem for men, whose friendships are usually less involved than those of women.

In short, emotional ties between the elderly and friends or neighbors may not be sufficiently strong to generate more than minimal aid.

Summary

Traditionally, the family, especially the adult children, has been the primary support system for the elderly, and it continues to provide such help today. Since the adult child's help to elderly parents appears to be limited in the light of present demographic, social, and economic trends, it is important, first, to clarify the role of adult children as helpers (that is, the degree and kinds of help they are able and willing to provide), and second, to clarify their role in a coordinated system of other service providers who also have their limitations. On the other hand, the adult child's help—regardless of limitations—is essential. It is important to determine any psychological characteristics of adult children that are related to helping behavior and which can be strengthened to sustain such helping behavior in the face of present-day societal trends.

Endnotes

1. V. G. Cicirelli, "Social Services for Elderly in Relation to the Kin Network," Report to the NRTA-AARP Andrus Foundation (1979).
2. S. E. Rix and T. Romashko, *With a Little Help from My Friends* (Washington, D.C.: American Institute for Research, 1980).
3. L. E. Troll and V. L. Bengtson, "Generations in the Family," in W. R. Burr, R. Hill, F. I. Nye, and I. L. Reiss (Eds.), *Contemporary Theories About the Family, Vol. I* (New York: The Free Press, 1979).
4. P. B. Baltes and S. J. Danish, "Intervention in Life-Span Development and Aging: Issues and Concepts," in R. R. Turner and H. W. Reese (Eds.), *Life-Span Developmental Psychology: Intervention* (New York: Academic Press, 1980), pp. 49–74.
5. H. L. Sterns and R. E. Sanders, "Training and Education of the Elderly," in R. R. Turner and H. W. Reese (Eds.), *Life-Span Developmental Psychology: Intervention* (New York: Academic Press, 1980), pp. 307–328.
6. B. R. Bild and R. J. Havighurst, "Family and Social Support," *The Gerontologist,* 16 (1976), pp. 63–69.
7. E. Litwak, "Geographical Mobility and Extended Family Cohesion," *American Sociological Review,* 25 (1960), pp. 9–21.
8. I. Rosow, *Social Integration of the Aged* (New York: Free Press, 1967).
9. E. Shanas, *Family Relationships of Older People* (Chicago: Health Information Foundation, 1961).
10. E. Shanas, "The Family as a Social Support in Old Age," *The Gerontologist,* 19 (1979), pp. 169–174.
11. E. Shanas and Associates, *Old People in Three Industrial Societies* (New York: American Press, 1968).
12. M. B. Sussman, "Relations of Adult Children with Their Parents in the United States," in E. Shanas and G. F. Streib (Eds.), *Social Structure and the Family: Generational Relations* (Englewood Cliffs, N.J.: Prentice-Hall, 1965).
13. L. E. Troll, "The Family of Later Life: A Decade Review," *Journal of Marriage and the Family,* 33 (1971), 263–290.

14. B. N. Adams, "Isolation, Function and Beyond: American Kinship in the 1980's," *Journal of Marriage and the Family*, 34 (1970), pp. 575–597.
15. M. H. Cantor, "Life Space and the Social Support System of the Inner City Elderly of New York," *The Gerontologist*, 15 (1975), pp. 23–27.
16. E. Shanas and G. Streib (Eds.), *Social Structures and the Family* (Englewood Cliffs, N.J.: Prentice-Hall, 1965).
17. J. Aldous, and R. Hill, "Social Cohesion, Lineage Type, and Inter-Generational Transmission," *Social Forces*, 43 (1965), pp. 471–482.
18. R. Hill, "Decision Making and the Family Life Cycle," in E. Shanas and G. F. Streib (Eds.), *Social Structures and the Family* (Englewood Cliffs, N.J.: Prentice-Hall, 1965).
19. B. N. Adams, "Structural Factors Affecting Parental Aid to Married Children," *Journal of Marriage and the Family*, 26 (1964), pp. 327–331.
20. B. Gibson, "Kin Family Network: Overheralded Structure in Past Conceptualization of Family Functioning," *Journal of Marriage and Family*, 34 (1972), pp. 13–32.
21. R. Hill, *Family Development in Three Generations* (Cambridge, Mass.: Schenkman, 1970).
22. E. Shanas, *The Health of Older People: A Social Survey* (Cambridge, Mass.: Harvard University Press, 1962).
23. E. Shanas, "Older People and Their Families: The New Pioneers," *Journal of Marriage and the Family*, 42 (1980), pp. 9–15.
24. H. E. Bracey, *In Retirement: Pensioners in Great Britain and the United States* (Baton Rouge: Louisiana State University Press, 1966).
25. M. B. Sussman and L. Burchinal, "Parental Aid to Married Children: Implications for Family Functioning," *Marriage and Family Living*, 24 (1962) pp. 320–332.
26. H. B. Brotman, *Who Are the Aged: A Demographic View* (Institute of Gerontology, University of Michigan, 1968).
27. S. Katz, "Anthropological Perspective on Aging," *The Annals of the American Academy of Political and Social Science*, 438 (1978), pp. 1–12.
28. E. Shanas and P. M. Hauser, "Zero Population Growth and the Family Life of Old People," *Journal of Social Issues*, 30 (1974), pp. 79–92.
29. M. R. Block, *Uncharted Territory: Issues and Concerns of Women Over 40* (Center on Aging, University of Maryland, 1978).
30. National Institute On Aging, *Our Future Selves: A Research Plan Toward Understanding Aging* (Washington, D.C.: DHEW, NIA, 1977).
31. J. Treas, "Family Support Systems for the Aged; Some Social and Demographic Considerations," *The Gerontologist*, 17 (1977), pp. 486–491.
32. United States Bureau of the Census, *Current Population Reports, P-23, No. 43; Projections of the Population of the United States, by Age and Sex* (Washington, D.C.: Government Printing Office, 1972).
33. D. E. Gelfand, J. K. Olsen, and M. R. Block, "Two Generations of Elderly in the Changing American Family: Implications for Family Services," *Family Coordinator*, 27 (1978), pp. 393–404.
34. B. E. Hess, and J. M. Waring, "Changing Patterns of Aging and Family Bonds in Later Life," *The Family Coordinator*, 27 (1978), pp. 303–314.

35. M. Petrowsky, "Marital Status, Sex, and the Social Networks of the Elderly," *Journal of Marriage and the Family,* 31 (1976), pp. 749–756.
36. R. A. Ward, "Limitations of the Family as a Supporting Institution in the Lives of the Aged," *The Family Coordinator,* 27 (1978), pp. 365–373.
37. L. Tiger, "Omigamy: The New Kinship System," *Psychology Today* (July, 1978), pp. 14–17.
38. W. H. Quinn and G. A. Hughston, "The Family as a Natural Support System for the Aged," Paper presented at the 32nd Annual Scientific Meeting of the Gerontological Society, Washington, D.C. (1979).
39. M. W. Riley and A. Foner, *Aging in Society, Vol. 1. An Inventory of Research Findings* (New York: Russell Sage Foundation, 1968).
40. B. E. Hess and J. M. Waring, "Changing Patterns of Aging and Family Bonds in Later Life," *The Family Coordinator,* 27 (1978), pp. 303–314.
41. M. Lowenthal and C. Haven, "Interaction and Adaptation: Intimacy as a Critical Variable," *American Sociological Review,* 33 (1968), pp. 20–31.
42. S. Sherman, "Patterns of Contacts for Residents of Age Segregated and Age Integrated Housing," *Journal of Gerontology,* 30 (1975), pp. 103–107.
43. J. Wax, "It's Like Your Own Home Here," *New York Times Magazine* (November 21, 1976), pp. 38 ff.
44. H. Lopata, *Widowhood in an American City* (Cambridge, Mass.: Schenkman, 1973).

Chapter 2

PERCEPTIONS, FEELINGS, AND BEHAVIOR PATTERNS: A BASIS FOR HELPING BEHAVIOR

To make possible maximum use of adult children as a support system means that their capability and willingness to provide services or helping behavior must increase. On a psychological level the question is: What psycho-social variables sustain or reactivate helping behavior of adult children toward their elderly parents over long time periods in the latter part of the parents' life span?

Troll and Bengtson[1] state that we must begin to explain this incredible long-lasting relationship among generations of the family. Since such helping behavior can be sustained over long time periods, great geographical distances, and in the face of considerable obstacles, one must assume that certain psychological factors endure within the individual over a life span and contribute to this kind of behavior.

Within this framework, certain variables are worth particular interest: attachment, attachment behavior(s), filial obligation, perceived conflict of adult children with elderly parents, and perceived dependency of elderly parents by adult children.

Attachment and Attachment Behavior

Attachment refers to an emotional or affectional bond between two people: it is essentially being identified with, in love with, and having the desire to be with another person. It is enduring and specific to a particular person.

19

According to some theorists, attachment represents an internal state within the individual. For example, Ainsworth[2] regards attachment as a stable propensity existing within the individual to seek proximity and contact with a specific individual. In this sense, attachment is a constant bond to the attached person. Once formed, it is always present, regardless of intervening distance or passage of time. (The strength of the bond varies from one person to another, depending on individual characteristics and life history.)

The existence of the attachment bond can be inferred from attachment behavior through which the individual seeks or maintains contact with the attachment object, although such behaviors may occur infrequently or intermittently. However, the attachment bond can be inferred from other independent indicators, especially with adults. (In a different context, Lamb[3] has argued that behavioral interaction is not necessarily an indicator of attachment but a consequence of it.) Attachment may be inferred from verbal reports about identification with the attached figure (for example, feelings of closeness, feelings of compatibility, etc.). In the present study, attachment is viewed as having properties of a motive, for example, the propensity to maintain contact and protect the attached figure.

The theory of attachment originated in the study of infants in the mother-infant relationship. The infant becomes attached to the mother out of a need to survive.

Attachment behavior, as distinguished from attachment, is an attempt by the infant or child to maintain proximity, contact, or communication with the discriminated attached figure (the mother). The infant or child will manifest reactions to initial separation, the length of time during separation, reunion after separation, and anticipated separation from or rejection by the attached figure. The infant or child may search, call, embrace, crawl, cling, hug, kiss, and so on to maintain or restore proximity, contact, and communication with the mother. Eventually, when the infant or child feels secure enough, exploratory behavior occurs in which the infant leaves the mother for varying distances and time periods to gain new experiences about the world. Attachment and exploratory behaviors alternate in time.

Finally, protective behavior develops in which the infant or child desires to protect the attached figure. That is, protective behavior is distinct from attachment behavior in that the former is concerned with preserving or restoring the threatened existence of the attached figure rather than maintaining or restoring proximity to the attached figure. Attachment and protective behavior are complementary to each other.

According to Bowlby,[4, 5] attachment to an attached figure, such as a mother or father, does not end in early childhood or adolescence. An attachment bond endures throughout the life span along with its concomitant attachment, exploratory, and protective behavioral systems. However, the forms of attachment, exploratory, and protective behavior change as one develops.

In adulthood attachment is manifested by attempting to be near or communicating periodically with the attached figure. The attachment behaviors are usually reactions to periods of separation (rather than reactions to initial separations, since most adult children do not live with their elderly parents) or are responses to reunions. Exploratory behavior is exemplified in mobility or migratory behavior. Adult children migrate for better jobs or for adventure, but their attachment manifests itself in their eventual return or periodic communication.

In addition, protective behavior is exemplified in the adult children's caregiving behaviors to their elderly parents. When the attachment bond is threatened by the elderly parents' illness or deprivation, the adult children provide caregiving to maintain the survival of the elderly parents and preserve the concomitant emotional bond.

The most basic indicator of the existence of an attachment bond is the adult child's feeling of closeness or affection for the elderly parent. Additionally, if attachment involves love, and identification with the other is an essential attribute of love, then the adult child should not only feel close to but have common values with the parent, perceive the parent positively, and feel compatible with the parent. Attachment behavior, by contrast, consists of residential proximity to the parents and frequent contact or communication, as indicated by visits, telephone calls, or letter writing. Protective or helping behavior, viewed as arising from the attachment bond, consists of the various services provided to the elderly parents by their adult children.

The concept of attachment behavior roughly corresponds to the concept of associational solidarity as used by various sociologists.[6] However, the concept of attachment seems more appropriate for a dyadic relationship on a psychological level, whereas the concept of solidarity has greater application for multiple relationships in a group on a sociological level. Secondly, in the psychological conceptual scheme, attachment as a bond is distinguished from attachment behaviors and from protective or helping behaviors, rather than all of these being attributes of the concept of solidarity. This allows these variables to be ordered meaningfully in terms of antecedent-consequent conditions.

At the present time, there is some inconsistency in the literature regarding the relationships between these variables. For example, Bengtson *et al.*[6] found empirical support for the notion that association (proximity and contact), affection, and value consensus were highly interrelated aspects of the single concept of solidarity. However, Troll and Bengtson[1] reviewed several studies which indicated that consensus was not significantly related to affection and association. They attempt to resolve this inconsistency by noting that perceived consensus but not actual consensus seems to be related to the other aspects of solidarity.

Adult Children's Feelings of Obligation Toward Parents

Not all relations between parents and their adult children are characterized by affection and close emotional ties. Many times, feelings of obligation or a sense of duty underlie helping behavior. Family loyalty is an important aspect in intergenerational relations.[7]

Some gerontologists feel that a role reversal often occurs between middle-aged adult children and their elderly parents. The middle-aged adult child takes the parental supportive role, while the elderly parent takes on the child's former dependency role. Such role reversals may be difficult for both individuals. The adult child may react with anger that the elderly parent is no longer the "strong one," and the elderly parent may react with hostility at having to be dependent upon the adult child. However, Blenkner[8] rejects this conception of conflict stemming from role reversal, and rejects the notion of role reversal itself, claiming that this happens only in pathological cases where both elderly parent and adult child have not continued their normal development in the life cycle.

Blenkner uses the term "filial maturity" or responsibility rather than role reversal. The adult child should not take on the parental role toward elderly parents, but should grow into a more mature filial role. During middle age, the adult child should begin to see the elderly parent as an individual, independent of being a parent; the adult child should identify with the elderly parent as an individual with personal needs and goals. This will be easier to do if the elderly parent has been a role model in the past, demonstrating mature filial behavior in relation to the adult child's grandparents.

When the adult child reaches filial maturity, the child willingly assumes a caretaking role for the elderly parents, and the parents come to realize that they can rely on the adult child without feeling hostility or rejection. The adult child thus changes in relation to the parents from the "emancipation-orientation" of younger adulthood and sees the parents in a mature way.[8]

Conflict Between Adult Children and Elderly Parents

Although feelings of affection and obligation toward elderly parents and perceptions of parental dependency by adult children may lead to increased helping behavior, one cannot exclude the existence of conflict between adult children and elderly parents as a possibly significant factor in reducing helping behavior.

The previous history of the quality of the relationship between adult children and elderly parents must be considered. If there has been a long history of rejection, alienation, or interpersonal conflicts, there may be little willingness for adult children to provide services or for elderly parents to accept them. Even appeals to affection or duty may induce little motivation.

However, another viewpoint[6,9] is that where strong positive feelings exist, strong negative feelings also exist. That is, love and hate can exist simultaneously in a relationship. If this is the case, then conflict between parent and child would not necessarily lessen helping behavior.

According to Horowitz,[10] a positive relationship with an elderly parent is not a necessary prerequisite for an adult child to provide care and help to that parent. Thus, it is unclear from the literature whether a relationship with a history of conflict between adult child and elderly parent would lead to increased or decreased helping behavior to the elderly parent, or even be unrelated.

Another aspect which must be considered is that conflict may lead not only to less helping behavior but to increased abusive behavior toward elderly parents. Although it may seem paradoxical that the family can be a source of love and care as well as a source of conflict and even violence, about a quarter of all homicides in the United States are committed by family members.

Perceived Dependency of Elderly Parent

An elderly dependent person is one who can no longer satisfy his needs or wants by himself; he needs help or support from others. According to Blenkner,[11] there are normal dependencies of old age which can be divided into economic (lack of finances), physical (diminished energy, poor health, slow reflexes, etc.), mental (deterioration in memory, loss of orientation, etc.), and social dependency (loss of roles, status, or power, etc.). Others should accept these dependencies of the elderly as real and be ready to provide help as needed.

However, some individuals or societies place too great an emphasis on self-reliance, and tend to perceive certain elderly people as too dependent, and, simultaneously, are unprepared to provide appropriate help.[12]

In this book, I attempt to obtain a measure of the adult children's perceptions of their elderly parents' degree of dependency, since it is felt that the perceived dependency (rather than the actual dependency) of the elderly parents will influence the adult children's helping behavior.

Effects of Background Variables: Socioeconomic Status, Sex, Age

The results of various studies of adult children's help to parents tend to be different or inconsistent, and many times such differences are related to background variables.

The socioeconomic status of the family appears to be an important factor in determining adult children's aid to elderly parents. Middle-class adult children tend to provide more financial aid (money, gifts, loans), while working class adult children provide more services.[7, 13, 14] Obviously, this is partially influenced by the fact that lower class adult children tend to live closer to their elderly parents. However, even if middle-class children live closer, they are often too busy in terms of more demanding professional occupations to provide direct services rather than financial aid. (Instead, they may hire someone else to provide the direct services.)

Middle-aged adult daughters tend to have closer relationships with their elderly parents than do sons.[15] Also, daughters traditionally provide more help to elderly parents than do sons,[16] particularly in areas of homemaking and personal care.

Lopata[17] found, in a study of the Chicago area, that widows' sons were helpful in practical matters, such as funeral arrangements and financial dealings, while their daughters fostered closer emotional ties by giving services and visiting.

While preparing a 1979 report,[18] I was struck by the fact that most elderly did not rely on a single kin member for services, but seemed to use the family member who was best fitted to give a particular kind of help. Thus, an elderly widow might get help from a daughter with homemaking, from a son with government and business dealings, from a grandchild with maintenance, from a sister with psychological support, and so on.

As increased numbers of women work and men take on more domestic duties, sex differences in help provided to elderly parents may be reduced. However, there is no clear indication that this is currently the case.

There is likely to be a wide age range among individuals with elderly parents, extending from early adulthood to early old age. A few elderly persons with minor children can be found. Yet, little is known of how adult children's feelings toward elderly parents may vary with age or how helping behaviors may vary. If Blenkner[8] is correct that filial maturity is attained sometime in middle adulthood, then one would also expect feelings and helping behaviors to change somewhat. In general, however, the ages of adult children and their elderly parents are correlated so that older adult children are more likely to have older parents with greater needs for services. Although studies of middle-aged adult children have found that they do feel close to their elderly parents,[9, 19] it is difficult to reach any conclusions about the age trend in children's feelings in middle adulthood toward elderly parents, since the different studies have dealt with different populations and have used different measures.

Additional Dependent Variables

Future Commitment to Help

Thus far, children's helping behaviors to elderly parents have been discussed in some detail. Yet, many elderly parents who are well past retirement age take care of their own needs and do not need help from their children or other service providers.[18] In all likelihood, however, most elderly parents will need help from others at a point when illness or other vicissitudes of aging become too great for them to handle alone. Often, adult children anticipate what their response to such future parental need will be, making statements to their elderly parents such as, "If you ever need help, call on me." Others might say, "I could help some, but can only do a little." Still others might say, "There is nothing I can do if that happens." Statements of this sort reflect a feeling of commitment on the part of the adult children as to the extent of help they would give in time of future need. If their commitment to help in the future is sincere and realistic, it will be translated into actual helping behavior when the need arises.

Stress Reactions

If elderly parents become dependent through ill health, loss of income in retirement, widowhood, or a combination of these factors, the balance of exchange of services between generations shifts, with adult children providing more help than they receive. Certainly a helping relationship can increase the affection of the caregiver and the emotional satisfaction of the receiver in being cared about, thus bringing family members closer together. However, if parental dependency becomes too great and helping behavior is carried too far, it may produce negative side effects.[10] Rosenmayr[20] has argued that help patterns should not in themselves be regarded as the criterion for a positive relationship between generations, for the stress caused by the care of the old has consequences on those providing the care.

For example, Adams[7] found that weaker affectional ties resulted when there was a one-way helping relationship from adult child to parents. Also, young to middle-aged adults who had widowed parents felt less close to that parent than did adults who had both parents living. Johnson and Bursk[19] found that adult children felt less positively toward their parents when the parents were no longer healthy and independent.

The needs of an aging dependent parent may result in stresses on adult children providing support and care.[9, 21] The media and clinical literature abound with anecdotal reports of personal strains and negative feelings experienced by adult children who bear a heavy load of responsibility in caring for dependent parents, becoming sufficiently severe in some cases as to lead to family breakdown or abuse of the elderly.[22, 23] A heavy load of responsibility may also inhibit or reduce further helping behavior and lead to rejection of the elderly parent and concomitant guilt in the adult child.

Model of Variables Influencing Helping Behavior

Figure 2-1 presents a model of hypothesized relations among the variables which have been discussed thus far. The adult child's feelings of attachment are regarded as antecedent to attachment behaviors, and, in turn, to present helping behaviors and future commitment to help. Filial obligation and historical conflict with the parent are also postulated to be related to attachment behaviors and, in turn, to present helping behaviors and future commitment to help. Perceived parental dependency is regarded as antecedent to present helping behaviors and future commitment to help. (Such characteristics of the adult child and elderly parent as age, sex, and socioeconomic status have not been included in the model, although they are considered to be related to attachment behaviors and present and future help.) Situational stress is seen as a consequence of present helping behaviors and may, in turn, act to reduce future commitment to help.

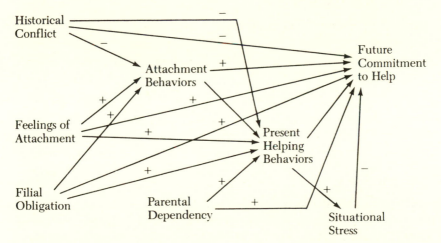

Figure 2-1   Model of Variables Influencing Adult Children's Present Help to Elderly Parents and Future Commitment to Help.

This model contrasts with the sociological model[6] which views closeness and helping behavior as merely aspects of a larger concept of parent-child solidarity.

Research Objectives

The general objective of this book is to determine the relationship between personal characteristics of adult children of elderly parents, characteristics of the parent-child relationship, and the adult children's views on providing services for elderly parents. More specifically:

1. To identify and describe certain demographic and personal characteristics of middle-aged adult children of the elderly;
2. To identify and describe certain demographic and personal characteristics of the elderly parents of these adult children;
3. To describe from the adult children's viewpoint the quality of their relationship to their elderly parents, that is, the adult children's perceptions, feelings, and behavior patterns toward their elderly parents;
4. To describe the adult children's views on what services they see as important for their parents, the extent to which they are supplying such services, and the kinds and amounts of services they are capable and willing to provide for their elderly parents in the future;
5. To determine the relationships between the characteristics of adult children and their parents, the quality of the parent-child relationships, and the adult children's views on services for their elderly parents.

It is hypothesized that the adult children's views on the kinds and amounts of services they are providing and are willing to provide for their elderly parents will vary with the quality of the relationship with (or their perceptions, feelings, and behavior patterns toward) their elderly parents, and with their own and their elderly parents' personal and dependency characteristics.

If such relationships can be demonstrated, it may be possible to modify some of these personal characteristics and feelings in order to enhance adult children's helping behavior. This book should help identify the strengths and limitations of adult children's capability for helping behavior, and clarify their role as service providers to their parents.

Endnotes

1. L. E. Troll and V. L. Bengtson, "Generations in the Family," in W. R. Burr, R. Hill, F. I. Nye, and I. L. Reiss (Eds.), *Contemporary Theories About the Family, Vol. I* (New York: The Free Press, 1979).
2. M. D. Ainsworth, "Attachment and Dependency: A Comparison," in J. L. Gewirtz (Ed.), *Attachment and Dependency* (New York: Wiley & Sons, 1972), pp. 97–137.
3. M. E. Lamb, "A Defense of the Concept of Attachment," *Human Development*, 17 (1974), pp. 376–385.
4. J. Bowlby, *The Making and Breaking of Affectional Bonds* (London: Tavistock Publications, 1979).
5. J. Bowlby, *Attachment and Loss, Vol. III, Loss: Stress and Depression* (New York: Basic Books, 1980).
6. V. L. Bengtson, E. G. Olander, and A. A. Haddad, "The Generation Gap and Aging Family Members: Toward A Conceptual Model," in J. F. Gubrium (Ed.), *Time, Roles, and Self in Old Age* (New York: Human Sciences Press, 1976).
7. B. N. Adams, *Kinship in an Urban Setting* (Chicago: Markham Publishing Company, 1968).
8. M. Blenkner, "Social Work and Family Relationships in Later Life with Some Thoughts on Filial Maturity," in E. Shanas and G. F. Streib (Eds.), *Social Structure and the Family* (Englewood Cliffs, N.J.: Prentice-Hall, 1965).
9. L. Troll, S. J. Miller, and R. C. Atchley, *Families in Later Life* (Belmont, Calif.: Wadsworth Publishing Company, 1979).
10. A. Horowitz, "Families Who Vary: A Study of Natural Support Systems of the Elderly." Paper presented at the 31st Annual Scientific Meeting, Gerontological Society, Dallas, Texas (November, 1978).
11. M. Blenkner, "The Normal Dependencies of Aging," in R. Kalish (Ed.), *The Dependencies of Old People* (Ann Arbor, Mich.: University of Michigan Institute of Gerontology, 1969).
12. R. Kastenbaum and P. Cameron, "Cognitive and Emotional Dependency in Later Life," in R. Kalish (Ed.), *The Dependencies of Old People* (Ann Arbor, Mich.: University of Michigan Institute of Gerontology, 1969).
13. E. Shanas and Associates, *Old People in Three Industrial Societies* (New York: American Press, 1968).
14. M. B. Sussman and L. Burchinal, "Parental Aid to Married Children: Implications for Family Functioning," *Marriage and Family Living*, 24 (1962), pp. 320–332.
15. L. E. Troll, "The Family of Later Life: A Decade Review," *Journal of Marriage and the Family*, 33 (1971), pp. 263–290.
16. M. B. Sussman, "Relations of Adult Children with Their Parents in the United States," in E. Shanas and G. G. Streib (Eds.), *Social Structure and the Family: Generational Relations* (New York: Prentice-Hall, 1965).

17. H. Lopata, *Widowhood in an American City* (Cambridge, Mass.: Schenkman, 1973).
18. V. G. Cicirelli, "Social Services for Elderly in Relation to the Kin Network," Report to the NRTA-AARP Andrus Foundation (1979).
19. E. Johnson, and B. J. Bursk, "Relationship Between the Elderly and Their Elderly Children," *The Gerontologist*, 17 (1977), pp. 90–96.
20. L. Rosenmayr, "The Family: A Source of Hope for the Elderly?" in E. Shanas and M. B. Sussman (Eds.), *Family, Bureaucracy, and the Elderly* (Durham, North Carolina: Duke University Press, 1977).
21. B. Robinson and M. Thurnher, "Taking Care of the Aged Parents: A Family Cycle Transition," *The Gerontologist*, 19 (1979), pp. 586–593.
22. M. R. Block and J. D. Sinnott (Eds.), *The Battered Elder Syndrome: An Exploratory Study* (College Park, Md., Center on Aging, University of Maryland, 1979).
23. S. K. Steinmetz, "Investigating Family Violence," *Journal of Home Economics*, Summer (1980), pp. 32–36.

Part Two

THE ANDRUS STUDY

Chapter 3

PLAN OF RESEARCH

In the attempt to answer the questions which were raised in the last chapter about adult children and their parents, we undertook a study of adult children. The study was essentially a field survey, in which we interviewed 164 adult children of elderly. To be included in the study, an individual had to have at least one living parent over 60 years of age, to reside within the city of Lafayette, Indiana, and be willing to take part in the study.

Site of the Study

The city of Lafayette, Indiana, where the study was carried out, is a small city with a population of approximately 50,000 persons. The city is located 60 miles to the northwest of Indianapolis, and 125 miles to the southeast of Chicago. This places it in one of the richest agricultural and industrial regions in the United States. Surrounded by farms specializing in production of corn and soy beans, the city supports a variety of industries. Notable among them are the manufacture of aluminum extrusion and tubings, electronics equipment, corn products, antibiotics, refined chemicals, prefabricated homes, animal feed products, and various food products. The city's growth has been moderate but steady over the past few decades. In spite of national economic problems, the current economic situation is mildly optimistic.

Just across the Wabash river, which bounds the city on the west, is the sister city of West Lafayette, which has a population of approximately 20,000 residents. West Lafayette is the home of Purdue University, a major school with some 30,000 students. The city of Lafayette has many service businesses catering to the university population as well as to its own residents. In addition, the university is itself a major employer in the greater Lafayette area.

While West Lafayette is a rather typical college town, Lafayette is distinctly different. The great majority of the residents are of northern European ancestry and are conservative in political views, religious beliefs, and life style. The availability of educational opportunities at Purdue University, as well as at a technical college, a business school, a nursing school, and three beauty schools, has led to a populace which is perhaps better educated than that of the average city of its size.

The population of the small midwestern city has been little studied in gerontological research, where most of the attention has been directed to large metropolitan areas. Yet the small city represents a way of life for millions of elderly Americans, and so is certainly worthy of study. A further reason for the selection of Lafayette as a site for the study was its convenience to Purdue University in West Lafayette, which permitted close monitoring and low costs for the study.

Obtaining the Sample

In carrying out the study, we wished to interview middle-aged adult children who had at least one parent still living. We used two means of locating this sample. Both were based on the method which was used in our recently completed study of elderly residents of Lafayette. Here, all residential blocks of the city were numbered, and a random sample was drawn. The field interviewers then canvassed each of the randomly sampled blocks to find and ultimately interview 300 elderly persons. Of these 300, there were 147 who had one or more children living in Lafayette. We were able to locate and interview 53 of the adult children of parents who had been interviewed in the earlier study. Although it was a relatively small group, we felt that it was an extremely important group to interview, since we could then directly compare the views of adult children with the views of their parents.

The remainder of our sample was obtained by contacting middle-aged adults in the blocks which had been canvassed earlier in the search for elderly residents. We located 111 adult children of elderly in this way. (We also obtained lists of middle-aged adults with elderly parents from local churches and other voluntary organizations;

by cross-checking these sources, we were able to assure ourselves that our sample was geographically representative of the city.)

Thus, we were able to obtain 164 completed interviews from a total of 288 contacts of adults who had at least one living parent over 60 years of age. This represents a completion rate of 57% overall. (Our least successful interviewer had a completion rate of 49%, while the most successful interviewer had a completion rate of 67%).

Constructing the Interview Questionnaire

In planning the interviews to be carried out with adult children of elderly, we were guided by the objectives of the study. Thus we first wanted to find out about the characteristics of the adult children whom we were interviewing and about the characteristics of their parents and siblings. Second, we wanted to know about the interpersonal relationships between adult children and their elderly parents. Third, we wanted to ascertain just how much help the adult children were giving their parents at present, as well as about the amount of help which they felt committed to provide at some future time when their parents' needs were greater. Finally, we wanted to explore some of the problems associated with helping elderly parents.

We were faced with a choice of planning either an interview in which we asked rather general open-ended questions or a more objective and tightly structured interview format. Each approach has certain advantages and disadvantages. The open-ended interview would allow us to explore more fully each interviewee's unique situation, feelings, and concerns about elderly parents, thus providing great richness of information. However, the data so obtained are difficult to code and analyze. Also, the success of the interview is dependent on the skill of the interviewer in gaining rapport with the individual to be interviewed, in knowing when to probe certain topics more fully, and in recording responses fully and objectively. By contrast, the structured interview format would permit a standardized set of questions for each person interviewed, with designated response alternatives for each question asked. With this approach, nearly all data coding could be completed at the time of the interview, with the data readily quantifiable for data analysis. This type of interview is less dependent on the skill and objectivity of the interviewer than is the open-end interview. However, since the structured interview is designed to explore only certain topics, some of the richness of the individual situation is not captured.

Of the two types of interview format, we selected the structured interview. We wished to be able to compare the responses of adult children with those of elderly parents, and the earlier study of the elderly used a structured interview format. Also, we wished to undertake a quantitative data analysis, and the structured format is more suitable for such a purpose.

An initial draft of the interview questionnaire was tried out on a small sample of adult children of elderly. This enabled us to detect any questionnaire items which were ambiguously worded, inappropriate, or ineffective, or which had poorly planned response alternatives. These items were modified accordingly. The revised interview questionnaire was again pilot-tested with a small group of middle-aged adults. One additional item was revised based on this experience, and the interview questionnaire was ready for use.

Selection and Training of Interviewers

Five research assistants carried out the field interviews of the adult children, although one of the five worked only during the summer. Three of the five were women and two were men; this gave us an approximate balance of the sexes of interviewers. Four of the five were graduate students in clinical psychology, and the fifth was a graduate student in the area of communications who had a research interest in interpersonal relationships in the clinical setting. All five had some previous experience in interviewing adults; one had worked on the previous project with elderly adults. All five had warm and friendly personalities, making it easy for them to establish rapport with the person to be interviewed.

Training of the interviewers consisted of several steps. First, general interview procedures were discussed. Then we went over the questionnaire, elaborating each item in detail so that the interviewers were familiar with the intent of each question and with the response alternatives. Ways of phrasing probing questions to clarify a response when needed were also illustrated. (In general, few probing questions were needed with the structured interview format.) Next, methods of recording responses were discussed. Then, interviewers administered the questionnaire to each other until they were fluent in the administration of the items and the recording of responses. At this point, trial interviews were arranged with volunteer subjects, with discussion and critique following each interview. The trial interviews were continued until we felt that each interviewer had reached a satisfactory level of competence. Finally, instruction was given in methods of locating prospective interviewees, securing consent for the interview, and reporting interviewing progress.

Interview Procedures

An interviewer went to the home of each prospective interviewee to make the initial contact. The individual was given a brief document describing the study, and the interviewer went over the description of the study in detail and answered any questions that might be raised. If the person agreed to be interviewed, the interviewer made an appointment for some convenient time to conduct the interview. Some people wished to be interviewed immediately, while others postponed it for a few weeks. Before the interview took place, the individual was asked to sign an Informed Consent form, in accordance with Purdue University and federal government procedures for the protection of human subjects. Such procedures were used to be sure that the prospective interviewee understood the purpose of the study, and was assured that adequate safeguards would be taken in the handling and reporting of the data to fully protect his or her privacy. Each person was instructed that he or she was to feel free not to answer particular questions or to withdraw from the interview at any time. (In actual practice, no one withdrew from an interview once it had started, and only one person declined to answer a few items. In contrast, most of the people interviewed seemed happy to talk about their relationships with their parents.)

During the interview, items were read in as conversational a tone as possible, and responses were immediately recorded on the interview questionnaire instrument. If an item did not appear to be clear to the interviewee, probing questions were asked, or the item was paraphrased. For certain groups of items, the interviewee was given a typewritten card containing the response alternatives for the item. This helped the person to concentrate on the content of the item without having to keep the response alternatives in mind. If need be, the interview was interrupted and concluded in a second session. However, this happened in only a few cases when an unexpected visitor arrived or the individual had to leave for another appointment.

The interview questionnaire was constructed to require approximately an hour and a half, although it was recognized that this time was likely to vary depending on whether one or both parents were living and on how many siblings there were. Also, some individuals were much more talkative than others. In fact, the average length of the interview was 93 minutes. However, interviews ranged from 40 to 225 minutes. The longest interview was with a garrulous person with a very large family.

Monitoring and Coding of Interviews

Each interview completed was reviewed within the week to detect any ambiguities or omissions in the data so that these could be rectified quickly. We were also available to answer questions and deal with any problems that arose in the field. In addition, we telephoned a small percentage of the adult children who were interviewed as a follow-up to determine whether there had been any problems with the interview and to thank them for their participation. This careful monitoring resulted in the virtual elimination of missing data problems and swift attention to any problems that arose in the field.

Coding of the data was carried out concurrently with the interviewing throughout the course of the project. Most of the coding was a mechanical task, in which preassigned numbers were attached to the response categories of the interview questionnaire.

The coding of occupational level was slightly more involved. The seven-point Hollingshead scale[2] was used to code the occupational data, with a "7" indicating the highest occupational level. Each occupation reported for an interviewee (or a family member) was matched to one of the seven categories of occupational titles provided by Hollingshead. For purposes of analysis, the occupational level of a husband and wife was taken as the highest occupational level attained by either spouse. The rationale for this procedure is that the occupational level tends to determine income level and life style of the family as well as the status accorded all the members. Since most employed women are at a lower occupational level than their husbands, and many other women are not employed outside the home, it is clear that for most families the husband's occupation is the primary determiner of the occupational status of the family.

To determine whether occupations could be coded reliably, two different coders worked independently to code a sample of 50 occupational titles reported in the interviews. The two coders agreed exactly on 94% of the occupational levels, and disagreed by no more than one level on the remaining 6%. Thus, we felt that the reliability of coding was quite satisfactory.

Differences Between Interviewers

We did not expect that the data obtained by the various interviewers would differ greater from interviewer to interviewer since the interview questionnaire was objective in nature. Also, the assignment of potential subjects to interviewers was random. Nevertheless, we carried out a one-way analysis of variance, with the five interviewers as the independent variable, to determine whether there were indeed differences between interviewers on a group of the items from the interview questionnaire. Fifty items representing the various sections of the interview questionnaire were selected for the analyses. Only two differences which were significant at the .05 level were found. Given the large number of analyses which were carried out, and the fact that the two differences were of borderline significance, we concluded that these findings were most probably due to chance. When similar analyses were carried out to compare male and female interviewers, no significant differences were found. On the basis of both types of analysis, we judged that there were no major differences in item responses due to interviewer.

Preparing Data for Analysis

We took several steps to insure that the data used for analyses were as error-free as possible. First, coded data were checked against the original interview forms at key points to guard against regularly recurring errors in coding. Next, all key-punching was independently verified. Finally, a computer check run was made in which responses for each item were examined to detect any data outside the normal range of variation expected for that item. When a response was found which was larger or smaller than expected, the original interview questionnaire was consulted in order to determine whether there was an error. A second computer check run was made to be sure that all errors had been corrected. At this point the data were considered ready for analysis.

Content of the Interview Questionnaire

We will now give a brief description of the interview questionnaire to better acquaint the reader with the type and scope of questions which were asked. The interview questionnaire consisted of several distinct parts: (1) the preinterview, (2) the personal-demographic information section, (3) the interpersonal relationships section, (4) the section dealing with services to the elderly, (5) special topics in regard to services, and (6) the postinterview.

The Preinterview

The preinterview consisted of two pages of preliminary data at the beginning of the interview questionnaire. Name, address, and telephone number of the middle-aged adult to be interviewed and of the elderly parents were requested. Sex of the interviewee was noted. The interviewer was identified on the cover page of the interview questionnaire by a code number. Also, the preinterview included the first of two rating items designed to get a measure of the vigor of the interviewee.[3] Here, the interviewer rated the general vitality of the person interviewed on the basis of the immediate impression of the person. The rating was made on a four-point scale ranging from "feeble" to "vigorous." The vigor measure which was used was a sum of this rating and a similar rating in the postinterview. It was felt that those middle-aged adults who were perceived as less vigorous might experience more difficulty in helping their elderly parents.

All information which provided identification of the person interviewed or of the elderly parents was contained on the first two pages of the interview questionnaire. After coding, these identifying pages were removed and replaced by an identification number in order that, in further data handling and storage, the privacy of the individuals concerned would be protected.

Personal-Demographic Information

This section of the interview questionnaire contained items that elicited personal and demographic information about the interviewees themselves, their elderly parents, and other family members.

Interviewees.   These items asked for age, marital status, religious preference, educational level, employment status, and occupational title of the middle-aged adult child of elderly parents. The educational level and occupation of the interviewee's husband or wife was also requested.

Children. We asked the middle-aged interviewees to report the total number of children they had, the number of these who were living at home, and the number who were still dependent on the middle-aged parents for support (whether or not they lived at home). We felt that those adult children who still had a heavy burden in raising or launching their own children would be less able to help elderly parents or would feel more stress in doing so.

Elderly Parents. The interview questionnaire contained sections concerned with each elderly parent individually, since in many cases only one parent was still living. We asked for each parent's age, employment status, level of education, and occupation. If the parent was retired, the occupation before retirement was used instead. Next, the living arrangements of the parent were probed. We asked whether the parent was living alone, living with a spouse, a child, or another family member, living in a retirement home or village, living in a nursing home or other type of institution, or whether there was some other type of living arrangement.

Another group of items dealt with the dependency of the parent. Perceived dependency of the parent was measured by asking the adult child to rate the extent to which the adult children of the family need to look after the parents now that they are getting older. A five-point scale ranging from "not at all" to "constantly" was used. Another item asked the interviewee to rate the extent to which the parent was viewed as dependent upon him or her. Again, a five-point scale was used, ranging from "not at all" to "very much." Further items were concerned with the parents' health. While we felt that parental health was not necessarily related to increased dependency, we wished to explore this question further as well as to provide a fuller description of the parents' situation. In one of the health items, the adult child was asked to rate the parent's state of health on a seven-point scale ranging from "excellent" to "critical." In another item the interviewee was asked what particular kinds of health problems the parent had, such as arthritis, diabetes, high blood pressure, cancer, and so on. We also asked whether the parent was under regular medical care, how adequate the parent's medical care was, and what problems in the parent's medical care were experienced.

Siblings. This section of the interview questionnaire dealt with

the siblings of the adult child who was interviewed. First, an enu-
meration of all siblings, living and dead, was obtained. Then sex, age,
birth order, educational level, and occupational information was obtained. (The interview questionnaire form provided space for data
regarding up to six siblings; for the few cases where there were more
than six siblings, additional pages from a second form were ap-
pended.)

Interpersonal Relationships

Items in this section were concerned with the relationship which
existed between the middle-aged adult children who were interviewed and their elderly parents. A number of aspects of the relationship were considered.

Attachment Behaviors. Two objective indicators of the child's
attachment to the parent are the proximity to the parent and the
amount of contact between child and parent. It is felt that these are
valid indicators of attachment in adulthood as well as in childhood.
In general, adult children who are strongly attached to their parents
will not be as likely to move to distant cities in search of employment
opportunities, and within the same city will be more likely to live in
the same neighborhood or even on the same block. Obviously, circumstances can act to alter or influence the expression of an adult
child's desire to live closer or further away from the parent, but on
the average those children with greater feelings of attachment will
live closer. Similarly, children with greater feelings of attachment
will have greater contact with their parents, both in terms of face-
to-face visiting and telephoning.

Three items in the interview questionnaire measured these attachment behaviors. Proximity was measured on a nine-point scale
ranging from "outside the continental United States" to "living with
interviewee." The amount of visiting and amount of telephoning
were each measured on a nine-point scale ranging from "not at all" to
"every day."

Feelings of Attachment. The subjective feelings which an adult
child has for an elderly parent are perhaps the most central aspect of
the parent-child relationship. An adult child may display attachment
behaviors due to circumstances, or out of a sense of duty, but the
subjective feelings represent the attachment bond which cements
and directs the relationship. Because of their subjective nature, they

are more difficult to assess. Therefore we included a number of
indicators of the adult child's feelings of attachment in the interview
questionnaire.

First, we included two items which had been used in a study of
younger adults by Adams.[4] Although these represented quite crude
measures, we had used them in our earlier study of the elderly[1] and
wished to be able to compare those findings to the results of the
present study. The first item asked the individual to express the
closeness of feeling toward the parent on a four-point scale ranging
from "not close at all" to "extremely close." The second item probed
the extent of value consensus with the parent by asking the adult
child to indicate the amount of agreement with the parent on "the
ideas and opinions about the things which you consider important in
life" on a four-point scale ranging from "don't agree at all" to "agree
completely."

Next, we included a group of six items to get at the adult child's
feelings of compatibility in the relationship with the parent. These
items dealt with the child's perception of the satisfaction gained from
the relationship with the elderly parent, how well the child gets
along with the parent, the degree of the parent's interest in the
child's concerns, the extent to which the parent likes to spend time
with the child, the extent to which the child feels free to ask intimate
questions or discuss intimate topics with the parent, and the extent
to which the child discusses important decisions with the parent.
Each item was measured on a five-point scale, with "1" representing
a low degree and "5" representing a high degree of the aspect of
compatibility probed by that item. In each case, appropriate anchors
for the five points on the scale were used which were in keeping
with the content of the item.

A group of twenty items asked for the child's perceptions of the
parent's personality traits. It was felt that adult children who had a
stronger attachment bond to the elderly parent would also identify
more strongly with the parent and would view the parent's personality traits more positively. The adult child was asked to indicate
the degree to which the parent possessed a given trait on a five-point
scale ranging from "very great degree" to "slight or not at all." The
twenty traits were taken from Itkin's intrafamily survey.[5] They were:
fair, selfish, envious, affectionate, helpful, sarcastic, considerate,
bossy, agreeable, kind, understanding, cold, suspicious, sympathetic, courteous, trustful, lazy, careless, dependable, and reasonable.

The scoring of these items was reversed for the negative personality traits so that a high item score referred to the most positive end of the scale in every case.

Conflict with the Parent.   Three items of the interview questionnaire probed the existence and extent of interpersonal conflict with the parent. The first of the three items asked the adult child to indicate the extent of present conflict with the parent on a five-point scale ranging from "none at all" to "almost every time you see each other." The second of the three items asked the adult child about particular areas which are sources of conflicts, such as the parent's criticism of the child's bad habits, the parent's criticism of the child's spouse, children, or friends, the parent's demands on the child, things the child thinks the parent should do, the parent's living arrangements, and so on. The third item asked about the extent of conflicts which would result if the parent lived with the child. The adult child was asked to respond on a six-point scale ranging from "none at all" to "conflict so severe it would never work."

Filial Obligation.   Since many gerontologists feel that much of an adult child's helping behavior in relation to elderly parents is motivated by a sense of duty or obligation, an adaptation of the filial expectancy scale of Seelbach and Sauer[6] was used as a measure of the adult child's sense of filial obligation. The scale consists of five items expressing behaviors commonly expected of adult children relative to their parents. The adult child was asked to indicate the extent of agreement with each item on a five-point scale ranging from "strongly agree" to "strongly disagree." The filial behaviors included in the scale are: living close to parents, taking care of parents when they are sick, visiting parents weekly, writing parents weekly if far away, and feeling responsible for parents. The scale score can range from 5 to 25 points and is obtained by summing the item scores. Low scores represent little filial obligation to the elderly parents and high scores represent high filial obligation. The scale was included in the interview questionnaire because it was felt that the child's sense of filial obligation would be related to the child's commitment to provide specific services to elderly parents.

Each of the items concerned with interpersonal relationships to elderly parents was administered in regard to fathers and then in regard to mothers. (The questionnaires also contained items dealing with the adult child's relationships with siblings. However, this material is not relevant to the main topic of this book and will not be discussed further.)

Services to Elderly Parents

A major section of the interview questionnaire was devoted to questions about the services which adult children and others provided to the elderly parents, about commitment to help in the future, about parents' needs for services, and about the importance of various services.

In our earlier study of the elderly,[1] we identified sixteen general types of services which elderly persons might perform for themselves or receive from their kin and other providers. Although we found that most elderly had little need for a few of these services, we included them all in the present study so that appropriate comparisons could be made between parents' and children's views on services.

One group of services was seen as of central importance to the continued existence and survival of all elderly persons. *Homemaking* services are needed in some degree by everyone. By this is meant such things as meal preparation, serving, and cleanup, shopping for food and other necessities, cleaning, laundry, and mending. Even when an elderly person lives in a retirement or nursing home, someone performs these basic tasks. When the elderly person lives at home in the community, he or she may perform these tasks independently, hire someone to do them, or receive help from children, other kin, friends, or neighbors. Similarly, regardless of where the elderly individual lives, there is either a direct or indirect reliance on some form of *maintenance* services. Included are repairs to the living quarters, such as plumbing; to electrical appliances, furniture, heating and cooling systems; and painting, papering, yard work, gardening, and so on. *Housing* services involve the provision of a house, apartment, or room to serve as individual or shared living quarters for the elderly person. *Income* services refers to the provision of either the money or the material goods and food needed for the elderly person to maintain the life style deemed necessary or desirable. The elderly person may still be employed or have some form of earnings, may rely on savings, may get Social Security payments, may get aid from welfare or other government agencies, or may receive funds or goods from children, other kin, friends, or neighbors.

Two other types of services can be regarded as of central importance to the survival of the elderly, although services from others may be needed only when the person's health becomes poor. First is *personal care* services, which includes such things as bathing, dressing, grooming, moving about the living quarters, and so on. Second, and related to the first, is *home health care* services. Such services as at-home treatments with special medicines, massages, exercises, other therapies, or home nursing care are examples of this type of service. The services may be performed by a member of the family, a friend or neighbor, or by a paraprofessional or professional medical person. Health care treatments at hospitals, clinics, doctors' offices, and so on are not considered here.

A second group of services helps the elderly person to maintain social interactions and participation in the life of the community. *Transportation* services provide a means of visiting friends, going out to meetings, taking care of business affairs, shopping, going to doctors, attending church, seeing family members, going to work, and any other activity which the older person might wish to undertake. All transportation beyond the block where the individual lives is considered within the context of transportation services, as is any form of transportation from walking to limousines. *Social and recreation* services include help with entertaining at home, visiting others, dining out with others, going to theaters, concerts, lectures, or sports events, attending meetings of organizations, outdoor activities such as sports or picnicking, and so on. If the elderly parents do not arrange social and recreation activities for themselves, then the adult children may create and arrange such activities for their parents. Or social and recreational activities for the elderly may be planned by voluntary organizations government agencies, friends, neighbors, and various kin. *Psychological support* services involve listening to and discussing problems and decisions with the elderly parents, giving understanding and advice, cheering up parents' spirits and otherwise improving morale, giving warmth, affection, respect, and being available for help. Such services can be given by a child or other family member, by friends or neighbors, or by professionals. *Spiritual* services include helping the elderly individual with attending church services, prayers, religious discussions, obtaining religious materials, and observing religious occasions. *Bureaucratic mediation* services for the elderly are concerned with getting information about programs or making applications to some government agency, arranging for some service, filling out forms, assisting in business and financial dealings, and so on. For many elderly individuals, bureaucratic red tape involved in transactions with government, banks, insurance companies, and business is highly complex or even baffling. Particularly when computers are involved, it may be a foreign world for the older person. Adult children, friends, neighbors, other kin, or professionals can act to "mediate" transactions of this sort. *Reading materials* services are related to the provision of such reading materials as books, magazines, pamphlets, or papers for the elderly person who is no longer able to acquire such things alone. The reading materials may be means for the elderly person to keep up on news, community events and problems, and social changes, or they may fulfill recreational needs. Adult children and other kin, friends, and neighbors may provide desired reading materials for the elderly parents. Voluntary organizations, community libraries, and the like may sponsor bookmobiles and other programs to provide reading materials to those elderly who can no longer obtain these things for themselves. Finally, *protective* services are those measures which protect the safety and security of the older individual. This may include checks on the person's health and well-being—daily or at other intervals—installing safety devices, instituting safety measures and precautions in the elderly parents' living quarters, protection against burglars and other criminals, and escorting the elderly in areas with a reasonable likelihood of crime or physical danger (icy streets, heavy traffic, stairs without handrails, and so on.)

A third group of services leads to personal growth of the elderly individual. These services may help the person to learn new things, or move in new directions in postretirement employment or career. *Employment* services help the elderly person to find a full- or part-time job, or to find a market for goods or services which the older person can supply. While these services are typically provided by government agencies and organizations for the elderly, families, friends and neighbors can also act in informal ways to help the older person find gainful work. *Career education* services are formal or informal education or training programs which prepare the elderly individual to enter some new occupation in later years. This may be a less complex or physically demanding job which allows for the declining vigor of old age, or it may mean a new career which allows the individual to satisfy new interests or reach changed goals. For example, a retired professor may move into real estate work after a period of training to obtain the necessary licensing. Or a bank teller may get further education to prepare him or her to aid taxpayers in completing income tax returns. Finally, *enrichment education* services enable the elderly parent to learn new things, develop special interests, and otherwise become able to live a richer, fuller life. They may learn new hobbies, arts, crafts, languages, health topics, religious studies, and so on.

The interview questionnaire contained a set of items for each of the sixteen types of services just described. The first of these items asked for the adult child's perception of the parents' need for the particular service. Responses were sought on a five-point scale ranging from "not at all" to "all of the time." Next the adult child was asked to indicate the amount of help which he or she gave the parents in this area, the amount of help which other siblings gave, and the amount of help from other kin. Responses were again on a five-point scale ranging from "none" to "all or almost all," where these refer to the amount of the service required to fill the parents' needs. The interviewee was asked to specify which sibling and which kin member provided the most help, if they did provide some help. The remaining items referred to a hypothetical future situation where the elderly parents needed a very great amount of help. The adult child was asked to indicate the amount of help which he or she felt committed to give the parents, and the amount of help expected from siblings, other relatives, government agencies, voluntary organizations, friends, neighbors, and hired help. The same five-point scale used for present services was used for future help. Again, interviewees were asked to specify the siblings and relatives expected to give the most help in the future. The items that probed future services were felt to be quite important, since many adult children felt that their elderly parents needed few or no services at the present time.

Additionally, the adult child was asked to rank the sixteen types of services in order of their importance to their elderly parents, and then to rank the sixteen services in the order in which he or she felt able to provide the most help to parents.

Special Topics

This section of the interview questionnaire was concerned with special topics related to adult children's provision of services to elderly parents.

One of the areas which we wished to explore in the study was the negative consequences for the adult child of helping the elderly parent. The burden of providing help to parents imposes a great deal of stress on many adult children. They report feeling tied down, "at the end of their rope," and not knowing where to turn for relief. We wished to determine the extent of such personal strains and negative feelings toward the parent among adult children in general.

We defined *personal strain* as a cognitive awareness of tension as a result of being unable to maintain a given situation or condition or accomplish a task. In the case of adult children, they may feel aware of such strains as a result of a burden of parent care which imposes stress upon them. On the basis of anecdotal reports of such strains found in the gerontological literature or in our own experience with aging families, we constructed a list of ten items which describe such personal strains. These were:

1. I feel physically worn out.
2. No matter what I do, my parent isn't satisfied.
3. It's causing a strain in my marriage.
4. It keeps me from helping my own children as I'd like.
5. I feel emotionally exhausted.
6. I have to give up social and recreation activities, vacations, and so on.
7. My job is being affected.
8. I feel tied down in my daily schedules.
9. It's causing a problem in my relationship with my children.
10. It's a real financial hardship for me.

The adult child was asked to respond to each item on a five-point scale, with response alternatives ranging from "not at all" to "very much," to indicate how each strain applied to him or her.

Similarly, we considered the *negative feelings* aroused by the stress of helping elderly parents. By negative feeling is meant an unpleasant emotional state. To obtain a measure of such negative feelings, we listed ten negative adjectives that describe the way many adult children feel when their aging parents require help and they are trying to give it. The words were: impatient, frustrated, helpless, bored, irritated, bitter, hopeless, resentful, guilty, and angry. The adult child was asked to indicate how much each emotional state was typical for him or her, on a five-point scale ranging from "not at all" to "very much."

Another special topic included in this section of the interview questionnaire was the extent of *sibling cooperation* in providing services to elderly parents. Five items were included to probe whether the adult child feels that brothers and sisters are doing their share in helping parents, whether they are dependable, whether it is possible to plan cooperatively with them to help parents, whether one sibling "takes over" too much, and whether the adult child feels "left out" by brothers and sisters when they help parents. Response to each item was on a five-point scale ranging from "no, not at all" to "yes, very much."

Finally, two open-ended items were included to permit the interviewees to respond more fully to the objective format of the remainder of the interview questionnaire. The first asked at what point, if any, the adult child felt that he or she could no longer continue to help an aging parent. The second item asked whether there were any problems in dealing with elderly parents or concerns about them which had not been taken up in the interview. This was included to give the adult child the opportunity to talk about idiosyncratic concerns.

Postinterview

This concluding section of the interview questionnaire was completed after leaving the interviewee. First, the interviewer completed the second part of the vigor rating begun in the preinterview. The adult child's energy level of both verbal and nonverbal behavior was rated on a four-point scale ranging from "low" to "high." Then the interviewer rated the respondent's attitude toward the interview, understanding of the questions, and any special circumstances surrounding the interview. These reports on the adult child's interview behavior made it possible to eliminate interviews from the analysis if the interviewee was hostile, didn't seem to understand the questions, or if there were any other conditions which might invalidate the interview. Fortunately, no such conditions were found. Finally, the interviewer noted the time and date, and the total length of the interview in minutes.

Derived Variables

Certain items from the interview questionnaire were combined to form derived variables for analysis. Discussion of these procedures will be treated in a later chapter where it is most appropriate.

Endnotes

1. V. G. Cicirelli, "Social Services for Elderly in Relation to the Kin Network." Report to the NRTA-AARP Andrus Foundation (May, 1979).
2. A. B. Hollingshead, "Two-factor Index of Social Position" (New Haven, Conn., 1957).
3. R. Kastenbaum and S. Sherwood, "Viro: A Scale for Assessing Interview Behavior." In D. P. Kent, R. Kastenbaum, and S. Sherwood, (Eds.), *Research Planning and Action for the Elderly* (New York: Behavioral Publications, 1972), pp. 166–200.
4. B. N. Adams, *Kinship in an Urban Setting* (Chicago: Markham Publishing Co, 1968).
5. W. Itkin, "Some Relationships Between Intra-family Attitudes and Preparental Attitudes Toward Children," *Journal of Genetic Psychology,* 80 (1952), 221–252.
6. W. Seelbach and W. Sauer, "Filial Responsibility Expectations and Morale Among Aged Persons," *Gerontologist,* 17 (1977), 421–425.

Chapter 4

ADULT CHILDREN AND THEIR ELDERLY PARENTS: A DESCRIPTIVE OVERVIEW

To give the reader a better understanding of the characteristics of the adult children who took part in the study and their elderly parents, the descriptive data elicited in the interviews is reviewed briefly. This background information will help to set the stage for the presentation of the study results and to provide a framework for their interpretation. By knowing the characteristics of the people who took part in the study, the reader will be better able to determine the extent to which the findings of the study apply to other similar cities and towns in the United States.

The Middle-Aged Adult Children

Of the 164 adults who took part in the study, 75 were men and 89 were women. Their ages ranged from 29 to 71 years. The mean age for the entire group was 46.4 years (SD = 8.7), while the mean age for men was 45.7 and for women 47.0 years. (The age difference between the two sexes was not statistically significant, however.) The number of men and women in each of four age groups is presented in Table 4-1. The mean for the age range 29–39 was 33.8 years, for the 40–49 age range was 44.5, for the 50–59 age range was 53.6, and for the 60–71 age range was 64.4 years.

The interviewer rated all persons in the study on their apparent vigor, using the Kastenbaum and Sherwood[1] scale. The scale values

Table 4-1   Numbers of Men and Women in Each of Four Age Groups

Age Group	Men	Women	Total
29–39	18	14	32
40–49	32	39	71
50–59	21	31	52
60–71	4	5	9
Total	75	89	164

could range from 0 to 6, with the highest score representing the greatest degree of vigor. The mean vigor rating for the adults of this study was 5.10 (SD = 1.16). Actually 92 of the 164 subjects (56%) had the top rating of "6," while only 11 (7%) had ratings of "3" or less. Thus, nearly all could be considered to be in good vigor.

In regard to marital status, the great majority 146 (89%) of the subjects of the study were married, 2 (1%) were widowed, 6 (4%) were divorced, and 10 (6%) were never married.

Most of the people participating in the study were high school graduates, and a majority had some further training beyond high school. Only 2 (1%) terminated their education at the elementary school level, 4 (2%) had some high school training, 49 (30%) were high school graduates, 52 (32%) had some vocational training or college work, 22 (13%) were college graduates, and 35 (21%) had some postgraduate training or advanced degrees. On the Hollingshead scale,[2] using "7" to represent the highest level of educational attainment, the mean educational level of the study respondents was 5.18 (SD = 1.21). The mean value indicates an educational level of some vocational training or college work after high school. The educational level of spouses of the study participants was similarly distributed. The relatively high educational level of the subjects of the study reflects the easy accessibility of college education for those in the local community who desire it.

Occupational level was also determined for the adult children in the study. Of the 164, 23 (14%) of the adult subjects of the study were unskilled, 5 (3%) were in semiskilled occupations, 24 (15%) were in skilled manual occupations, 34 (21%) were clerical workers, sales clerks, technicians, or little business owners, 43 (26%) were administrative personnel, small business owners, or semiprofessionals, 22 (13%) were business managers, owners of medium-sized businesses, and lesser professionals, and 13 (8%) were major professionals, higher executives, or owners of large businesses. The mean occupational level on the Hollingshead scale[2] was 4.14 (SD = 1.74), with "7" representing the highest occupational level. This mean represents an occupational status level of clerical workers, sales clerks, technicians, or little business owners. The occupational level of the 146 spouses of the interviewees was distributed similarly to that of the interviewees themselves, For purposes of analysis, the occupational level of the household was taken as the higher occupational level attained by either spouse. (In most cases, the husband's occupation determined the occupational level of the household.) The rationale for this was that the higher of the occupational levels provided the best indicator of the life style of the household.

Overall, 75% of the 164 middle-aged adults who were interviewed were employed either full or part time. However, since women are less likely to be employed outside the home, employment status was examined separately for men and for women. Among the 75 men, 68 (91%) were employed full time, 1 (1%) was employed part time (1–34 hours per week), 4 (5%) were unemployed or unable to work, and 2 (3%) were retired. Among the 89 women, 40 (45%) were employed full time, 14 (16%) were employed part time, 7 (8%) were unemployed, 2 (2%) were retired, and 26 (29%) were housewives. The employment status of the spouses of the adults interviewed was similar to the distribution for interviewees of the same sex. In general, almost all men were employed either full or part time, as were more than half of the women.

When the number of working women interviewees was considered along with the number of working wives of male interviewees, 58% of all households represented in the study had a woman who was employed either full time or part time outside the home. If the number who were temporarily unemployed was also taken into account, almost two-thirds of all households had a working woman. It is clear that the national trend for women to enter the work force extends to the small midwestern city as well.

In terms of religious preference, 59% of the subjects of the study were Protestant, 29% were Catholic, 5% were Jewish, 5% were of other faiths, and 2% had no preference.

Some 91% of the 164 middle-aged adults participating in the study had one or more children. The mean number of children was 2.81 (SD = 1.62). Only 1.48 children were still living at home, on the average, and only 1.45 were still receiving some form of support from their middle-aged parents. Looking at these data from another perspective, 30% of the interviewees had no child still remaining in the home.

The number of children still living at home declined with increasing age of their middle-aged parents, as might be expected. In the 50–59 age group, the mean number of children at home was 0.81, while in the 60–71 age group, it was only 0.33.

Brothers and Sisters

Each person participating in the study was asked to list all brothers and sisters, living or dead. The percentage of the 164 interviewees with various numbers of siblings of a given type is presented in Table 4-2. In the table, 12% of the study participants were "only" children, while 88% had one or more siblings. However, by the time of the study, only 85% had living siblings. The group had a mean of 1.04 living brothers and 1.13 living sisters. Some 60% had one or more living brothers and 62% had one or more living sisters. The most frequent family size was one sibling, followed closely by two siblings. Only 12% had five or more brothers and sisters.

The number of siblings and number of living siblings were examined separately for each age group; however, there were no significant age trends.

Of the 164 middle-aged adults studied, 77 (47%) were first-born children in their family of origin. An additional 41 (25%) were second-born children, 26 (16%) were third-born children, and 19 (11%) were born into fourth or higher positions. When the interviewees were categorized into three major birth-order groups, there were 47% first borns, 29% middle borns, and 24% last borns.

Sibling age covered a wide range, as did the age of the subjects of the study. Age of the oldest sibling ranged from 31 to 69 years, with a mean of 46.77 years. For the second sibling, age ranged from 26 to 67, with a mean of 44.60 years. For the third sibling, age ranged

Table 4-2 Percentages of Adults with Different Numbers of Siblings

Group	Number of Siblings						Mean	SD
	0	1	2	3	4	≤5		
Living brothers	40	35	16	5	2	3	1.04	1.21
Brothers born	31	41	16	7	3	3	1.19	1.25
Living sisters	38	30	23	5	2	3	1.13	1.25
Sisters born	35	31	23	7	1	4	1.21	1.30
Living siblings	15	30	23	15	7	11	2.18	2.02
Siblings born	12	27	24	16	10	12	2.39	2.04

from 23 to 63 with a mean of 41.90 years. Mean ages for the fourth, fifth, and sixth siblings were 41.18, 41.74, and 38.39 years, indicating a decline in mean age for later-born siblings.

In terms of education and occupational levels, siblings were closely similar to the subjects of the study, although mean levels declined somewhat for later-born siblings. This is most probably associated with the difference in age between successive siblings, since the younger siblings have had less time for career advancement and additional education.

Elderly Fathers

All 164 study participants had at least one living parent. However, only 81 had living fathers. Of the 81, 65 (80%) were married and 16 (20%) were widowed.

Age of the fathers ranged from 60 to 95, with 24 (30%) in the 60–69 age range, 36 (44%) in the 70–79 age range, and 21 (26%) age 80 and over. Mean age for the group of fathers was 74.14 years (SD = 7.60).

As anticipated, most of the elderly fathers of the interviewees were retired. Retirees numbered 65 of 81 (80%). Only 9 (11%) were working full time, 5 (6%) were working part time, and 2 (2%) were unemployed.

Interviewees were asked about the father's occupation when he was working (or if working after retirement, for his last career occupation). There were 9 (11%) who had been in unskilled occupations, 10 (12%) in semiskilled occupations, 22 (27%) in skilled manual occupations, 3 (4%) in clerical or technical positions, 29 (36%) were administrative personnel, small business owners, or semiprofessionals, 5 (6%) were business managers, owners of medium-sized businesses, and lesser professionals, and 3 (4%) were higher executives, owners of large businesses, or major professionals. The most frequent types of occupation were administrative personnel, small business owners, or semiprofessionals, followed closely by skilled manual occupations. The mean occupational level for the 81 fathers was 3.74 (SD = 1.63), with the mean above the skilled manual level but below the clerical and technical level. Thus, the occupational level of the fathers was somewhat lower than that of the interviewees themselves, whose mean occupational level was at the administrative personnel, business owner, and semiprofessional level.

The educational level of the 81 elderly fathers ranged from the elementary grade level to postgraduate training. There were 11 (14%) whose education terminated at the sixth grade or before, 20 (25%) at the seventh to ninth grade level, 10 (12%) with some high school work, 18 (22%) high school graduates, 12 (15%) with some college or vocational training, 7 (9%) college graduates, and 3 (4%) with postgraduate training or advanced degrees. The mean educational level was 3.41 (SD = 1.69), at the level of some high school work. Elderly fathers were clearly at a lower educational level than their adult children who had, on the average, some college or vocational training.

Most of the elderly fathers—72 of the 81 (89%)—lived in their own homes either alone or with their wives. Of the remainder, 4 (5%) lived with the adult child who was interviewed, 1 (1%) lived with a brother or sister, and 4 (5%) lived in a retirement home apartment. None were living in hospitals, nursing homes, or other institutions.

The adult child who was interviewed was asked to indicate the state of the elderly father's health on a seven-point scale ranging from excellent ("7") to critical ("1"). Of the 81 fathers, 11 (14%) were in excellent health, 14 (17%) in very good health, 35 (43%) in good health, 6 (7%) in not-so-good health, 10 (12%) in poor health, and 5 (6%) in very poor health. Most children (74%) felt that their fathers were in good, very good, or excellent health. The mean health rating was 4.94 (SD = 1.36), approximately at the "good" health level.

When the adult child was asked to enumerate the father's specific health problems, from 0 to 6 problems were listed. The average was 2.16 (SD =1.57) problems for each elderly father. The percentages of fathers with specific health problems were as follows: arthritis, 23%; diabetes, 11%; high blood pressure, 23%; heart disease, 33%; cancer, 9%; emphysema, 14%; vision problems, 37%; hearing problems, 32%; senility, 11%; and assorted other problems, 22% (such other problems as circulatory problems, thyroid, obesity, gout, kidney disease, hernia, foot problems, blood clots, loss of balance, and crippled limbs). Only 17% reported no problems. It is remarkable that in spite of this variety of health problems, so many elderly fathers were considered to be in "good" health or better by their adult children.

Some 26% of the 81 elderly fathers were under frequent, regular, medical care, 33% were under regular but occasional medical care, and 41% rarely, if ever, saw a doctor. When those adult children whose fathers received at least occasional care were asked to rate the adequacy of the medical care received, 40% regarded the care as very good, 47% regarded it as good, 10% saw it as fair, and only 3% felt that their fathers received poor medical care. The adult children were also asked about specific problems associated with the process of getting medical care for their fathers. While 52% saw no problems, the rest identified from one to four areas of concern. These included such things as: father won't go to doctor, 10%; father won't follow doctor's advice, 11%; high cost of care, 11%; transportation difficulties, 2%; inability to find any medical treatment to relieve his condition, 11%; needs someone to give medication or treatments at home, 2%; doctor won't come to house, 11%; hard to get appointments with doctor, 4%; doctor rushed and doesn't explain things, 14%; doctor has negative attitude toward elderly patients, 2%; and other assorted problems, 5% (for example, father doesn't ask doctor questions, has different doctor than mother, inadequate stair rails in doctor's office). Thus, the majority of elderly fathers were under some type of regular medical care. Most children saw this care as good or very good, but almost half found some areas of concern in the medical care process.

Elderly Mothers

Of the 164 adult children of elderly who participated in the study, 148 had living mothers; 65 (44%) of these were married and 83 (56%) were widowed.

Age of the elderly mothers ranged from 55 to 93. (Although one selection criterion for study participants was to have a living parent over age 60, there were a few mothers under age 60 who were married to older men.) By age group, 45 of the mothers (30%) were in the 55–69 age range, 64 (43%) were in the 70–79 age range, and 39 (26%) were aged 80 and over. Mean age for the group of mothers was 74.07 years (SD = 8.23). Although the mean ages of the elderly mothers and elderly fathers were almost the same, the standard deviations indicate that the mothers were slightly more variable in age than the fathers.

In regard to employment, 124 of 148 elderly mothers (83%) were housewives, although 36% had retired from a job some time previously. In addition, 11 (7%) were working full time, 4 (3%) were working part time, and 3 (2%) were unemployed and seeking work. There were 6 elderly mothers who were incapacitated and unable to work or to assume housewifely duties.

When adult children were asked for the mother's occupation at a time when she was last working (or, if working after retirement, for her last career occupation): there were 75 (51%) who had worked in unskilled occupations (including housewives), 19 (13%) in semi-skilled occupations, 6 (4%) in skilled manual occupations, 30 (20%) in clerical, technical, or sales clerical positions, 10 (7%) in administrative or semiprofessional positions or small business owners, 7 (5%) in business managerial positions, lesser professionals, or owners of medium-sized businesses, and 1 (1%) in a major professional position. Thus, most of the elderly mothers were either housewives or had worked in an unskilled occupation. The mean occupational level for the 148 mothers was 2.36 (SD = 1.67). This reflected a semiskilled level on the average, and was considerably lower than the occupational level of the elderly fathers or of their middle-aged adult children.

Educational level of the 148 elderly mothers was also determined: 13 (9%) had no more than a sixth grade education, 33 (22%) completed grades seven to nine, 26 (18%) had some high school work, 50 (34%) completed high school, 18 (12%) had some college or vocational training, 6 (4%) were college graduates, and 2 (1%) had postgraduate training or an advanced degree. The most frequent educational level was that of high school graduate; only about a third of the group attained this level. The mean education level of the elderly mothers was 3.36 (SD = 1.37), at the level of some high school work. Thus, the mean educational level of the elderly mothers was quite similar to that of the elderly fathers, although both parents were less well educated than their middle-aged adult children.

The great majority of the 148 elderly mothers, 110 (74%), lived in their own homes either alone or with their husbands. In addition, 16 (11%) lived with the child who was interviewed, 1 (1%) lived with another child, 2 (1%) lived with a sibling, 1 (1%) lived with friend, 11 (7%) lived in a retirement home or retirement apartment, 6 (4%) lived in a nursing home or other institution, and 1 (1%) alternated between the homes of several children.

As for the elderly fathers, the adult child was asked to indicate the state of the mother's health on a seven-point scale ranging from excellent to critical. Of the 148 mothers, 19 (13%) were considered to be in excellent health, 20 (14%) were in very good health, 56 (38%) were in good health, 23 (16%) were in not-so-good health, 10 (13%) were in poor health, 10 (7%) were in very poor health, and 1 (1%) was in critical health. Here, some 65% of elderly mothers were seen to be in good, very good, or excellent health. By comparison, 74% of elderly fathers were in good health or better. The mean health rating was 4.75 (SD = 1.41), slightly below the "good" health level. Also, the mean health of the elderly mothers was slightly poorer than that of the elderly fathers.

When the adult children enumerated the elderly mothers' specific health problems, from 0–8 problems were listed, with an average of 2.64 (SD = 3.14) problems for each elderly mother. The percentages of mothers with specific problems were as follows: arthritis, 69 (47%); diabetes, 16 (11%); high blood pressure, 73 (49%); heart disease, 35 (24%); cancer, 10 (7%); emphysema, 9 (6%); vision problems, 46 (31%); hearing problems, 35 (24%); senility, 15 (10%); and assorted other problems, 52 (35%). The "other problems" included a host of complaints such as problems with circulation, kidney, bladder, gall bladder, bowel, stomach, foot, inner ear, hernia, muscle deterioration, Parkinson's disease, hepatitis, osteoporosis, gout, bursitis, stroke, lung infection, allergy, depression, nervous complaints, and hypochondria. The incidence of arthritis and high blood pressure reported for elderly mothers was almost twice as great as that reported for elderly fathers; mothers had substantially more assorted complaints than did the fathers. However, elderly mothers had a lower incidence of heart disease, emphysema, and vision and hearing problems than elderly fathers.

Some 46% of the elderly mothers were under frequent, regular, medical care; 37% were under regular but occasional medical care; and 17% rarely, if ever, saw a doctor. It is unclear whether the elderly mothers' greater number of medical problems is responsible for the greater percentages who are under medical care than was the case with the elderly fathers, or whether the elderly mothers' propensity to see doctors merely results in the identification of more health problems.

When the adult children were asked to rate the adequacy of the medical care their mothers were receiving (for those mothers who received at least occasional care), 46% regarded the care as very good, 39% regarded it as good, 14% regarded it as fair, and only 1% regarded it as poor. The adult children were also asked about specific problems associated with the process of getting medical care for their mothers. While 51% reported no problems, the rest named up to six areas of concern. These included such things as: mother won't go to doctor, 11%; won't follow doctor's advice, 11%; high cost of care, 10%; transportation difficulties, 11%; inability to find any medical treatment to relieve her condition, 11%; mother needs someone to give medication or treatments at home, 5%; doctor won't come to house, 12%; doctor has negative attitude to elderly patients, 5%; and other assorted problems, 7% (e.g., communication problems with doctor, mother won't admit problems, illnesses keep recurring, long periods in waiting rooms to get care, problems with insurance claims, difficulty in finding doctor, conflict between doctor and nursing home, mother and father have different doctors). There was only one area in which adult children saw mothers as having substantially more problems associated with medical care than did fathers; this was concerned with transportation difficulties. Given the greater proportion of elderly mothers who were widowed, this is not surprising.

Summary

The detailed data which have been presented in this chapter to describe the adult children who were the subjects of the study and their elderly parents can be summarized to yield a composite portrait of the average interviewee.

The study participants were 75 men and 89 women, ranging in age from 29 to 71; 89% were married. The average interviewee was 46.3 years old, and was in relatively vigorous health. He or she had some college work or vocational training after high school graduation, and was working in a clerical job, as a technician, or as a salesclerk. Some 91% of the men and 45% of the women worked full time. When both full- and part-time jobs were considered, 58% of all the households interviewed had a woman in the work force. In regard to religious preference, 59% of the participants were Protestant, 29% Catholic, and the remainder of Jewish and other faiths or without religious preference.

The average interviewee had 2.81 children, of whom 1.48 were still living at home and 1.45 were still receiving some kind of support. Only 30% had a completely "empty nest."

Most study participants came from two- or three-child families; 85% had one or more living siblings at the time of the study. The average interviewee had 1.04 living brothers and 1.13 living sisters. Only 12% had five or more brothers and sisters. When categorized into birth-order groups, 47% of the interviewees were first born, 29% were middle born, and 24% were last-born children in their families of origin. Siblings tended to be similar in age, education, and occupational level to the study participants, although there was a decline noted for later-born siblings.

The subjects of the study had 81 living elderly fathers and 148 living elderly mothers. Some 80% of the fathers were still married, and 56% of the mothers were widowed. The age of the average parent was 74 years. He or she had some high school education. The average father was likely to have worked in a skilled manual occupation, while the mother was most likely to be a housewife. Most of the elderly parents were retired, and were still living in their own homes either alone or with their spouses. The overall health of elderly parents was seen as good by their adult children in spite of a variety of health problems.

Endnotes

1. R. Kastenbaum and S. Sherwood, "Viro: A Scale for Assessing Interview Behavior." In D. P. Kent, R. Kastenbaum, and S. Sherwood, (Eds.), *Research Planning and Action for the Elderly* (New York: Behavioral Publications, 1972), pp. 166–200.
2. A. B. Hollingshead, "Two-factor Index of Social Position" (New Haven, Conn., 1957).

Chapter 5

ADULT CHILDREN'S VIEWS ON SERVICES FOR ELDERLY PARENTS

Since an earlier study[1] revealed that elderly parents, when help was needed, preferred to receive most types of help from their adult children, one of the major objectives of the present study was to determine how adult children of the elderly felt about providing services to their parents. A secondary objective was to find out how the adult children felt about their parents' obtaining services from other providers.

The adult children were asked about several aspects of services for elderly parents in the interview questionnaire. First, they were asked about their elderly parents' needs for various types of service at the present time. Next, they were asked about how much help they gave their parents at present, as well as how much help their brothers and sisters and various other kin gave these elderly family members. Finally, the adult children were asked about a hypothetical future situation when their parents would be in need of a great deal of help. They were asked to indicate the extent of their own commitment to help and about the amounts of help expected from siblings, other kin, government agencies, voluntary organizations, friends, neighbors, and hired service providers.

Each of sixteen types of service was considered in turn. The parents' needs for services, and the amount of present and expected future services from the adult children and other service providers, was determined for each type. The sixteen types of service, which were discussed more fully in Chapter 3, are as follows:

Homemaking—involving meals, shopping, cleaning, etc.

Housing—providing living quarters

Maintenance—yard work, household repairs, etc.

Income—money, food, or goods needed to live on

Personal care—bathing, dressing, grooming, moving about

Home health care—at-home medical or health treatments or home nursing care

Transportation—means of getting to work, shopping, church, doctors, visiting, etc.

Social and recreational activities—entertaining at home, going out to special events, meetings, etc.

Psychological support—listening to problems, giving understanding and affection, etc.

Employment—finding a job or a market for goods and services

Spiritual—church services, prayers, religious observances, etc.

Bureaucratic mediation—dealings with government agencies, businesses, etc.

Reading materials—books, magazines, papers, etc.

Career education—training or education for a new job or career

Enrichment—learning new hobbies, arts, crafts, special interests, etc.

Protection—guarding against crime or danger, checks on daily health and security

In this chapter, the adult children's views on these sixteen types of service will be presented.

Parents' Needs for Services

The adult child who was interviewed indicated the degree of the parents' need for each type of service on a five-point scale ranging from "not at all" to "all the time." The percentages of adult children placing their parents' needs for each type of service in the five response categories are presented in Table 5-1.

The percentage of adult children who see their parents as having *no* needs for services at the present time is of considerable interest. This percentage indicates those who see their parents as being completely able to take care of all their needs in a particular service area; that is, those whose parents are independent. The highest percentages (indicating the areas in which most children saw their parents as needing no services from others) were found for career education

Table 5-1   Adult Children's Perceptions of Elderly Parents' Needs for Services in 16 Service Areas: Group Means and Response Frequencies

Type of Service	Mean	SD	Percentage of Responses				
			Not at all	On rare occasion	Fre- quently	Most of the time	All of the time
Homemaking	2.02	1.33	53	17	13	7	9
Housing	1.46	1.20	85	2	2	2	9
Income	1.17	0.58	91	3	4	2	0
Maintenance	2.57	1.44	34	17	22	12	15
Personal care	1.41	0.94	79	10	5	3	3
Home health care	1.43	1.01	81	6	5	4	4
Transportation	2.42	1.66	49	13	8	7	23
Psychological support	2.43	0.95	16	39	34	9	2
Social and recreation	1.54	1.04	72	13	8	4	4
Employment	1.05	0.36	98	1	1	0	1
Spiritual	1.58	0.96	66	15	13	3	2
Bureaucratic mediation	2.22	1.41	46	18	16	8	12
Reading	1.32	0.86	85	4	7	1	2
Career education	1.02	0.22	99	0	1	0	0
Enrichment	1.49	0.94	71	17	6	2	3
Protection	2.01	1.26	50	21	15	8	7
Total service need	27.15	9.18	—	—	—	—	—

(99%), employment (98%), income (91%), reading materials (85%), and housing (85%). The lowest percentages (indicating areas in which the majority of adult children saw their parents as needing some degree of services or, conversely, in which a minority of adult children saw their parents as needing no services from others) were found for psychological support (16%), maintenance (34%), bureaucratic mediation (46%), transportation (49%), and protection (50%). For the remainder of the service areas, a majority of adult children saw their parents as having no need for service; these areas were homemaking (53%), spiritual (66%), social and recreation (72%), enrichment (71%), personal care (79%), and home health care (81%).

Looking at the other end of the response scale, from 0% to 23% of adult children viewed their parents as needing help from others for *all* their needs, depending on the type of service involved. The highest percentages were found for transportation (23%), maintenance (15%), bureaucratic mediation (12%), homemaking (9%), and housing (9%).

Means and standard deviations for the elderly parents' needs for services for each of the 16 types of services are also presented in Table 5-1. These means range from 1.02, representing almost no need for service, to 2.57, representing a level of need between rare and frequent. The adult children, on the average, viewed their parents as having the greatest needs for service in the area of home maintenance (M = 2.57), followed by psychological support (M = 2.43), transportation (M = 2.42), bureaucratic mediation (M = 2.22), homemaking (M = 2.22), and protection (M = 2.01). The lowest needs for service were seen in the areas of career education (M = 1.02), employment (M = 1.05), income (M = 1.17), and reading materials (M = 1.32).

With the aim of constructing one or more summary scores to represent parents' needs for services for purposes of analysis, a factor analysis of the scores for the 16 types of services was carried out. Results indicated a single general factor. Therefore, a total score was constructed by summing the scores for the 16 service areas. The mean for the total service need score was 27.15 (SD = 9.18). Taken over all types of service, this indicates that on the average adult children felt that their parents needed help only rarely.

Help From Adult Children

Adult children were asked how much help they gave their parents at the present time for each of the 16 types of service. On a five-point scale, responses ranged from "none" to "all or almost all" of the parents' needs. Data summarizing adult children's provision of services to their elderly parents are presented in Table 5-2.

The percentage of adult children providing *no* service to their parents ranged from 9% to 99% over the 16 types of services. The highest percentages (indicating that most of the adult children provided no service) were in the areas of employment (99%), career education (99%), housing (87%), income (87%), home health care (85%), and personal care (84%). The lowest percentages (indicating that fewer adult children provided *no* service and, conversely, that more adult children provided some degree of service to parents) were found for psychological support (9%), maintenance (45%), homemaking (54%), transportation (55%), protection (55%), and bureaucratic mediation (56%).

Looking at the other end of the response scale, the service areas where the highest percentages of adult children provided all or almost all of the parents' needs for the service were transportation (10%), housing (10%), maintenance (8%), and bureaucratic media-

Table 5-2   Amount of Help Provided by Adult Children to Elderly Parents in 16 Service Areas: Group Means and Response Frequencies

			Percentage of Responses			
Type of Service	Mean	SD	None	Occa-sional help	Some reg. help	Great deal help	All or almost all
Homemaking	1.79	1.10	54	26	11	4	5
Housing	1.45	1.22	87	1	2	0	10
Income	1.10	0.50	87	8	5	0	0
Maintenance	2.11	1.30	45	25	12	10	8
Personal care	1.26	0.72	84	12	1	2	1
Home health care	1.27	0.78	85	8	4	1	2
Transportation	2.03	1.40	55	18	6	10	10
Psychological support	2.73	0.96	9	33	36	20	2
Social and recreation	1.60	1.00	66	18	10	3	3
Employment	1.03	0.32	99	1	0	0	1
Spiritual	1.54	0.99	70	16	9	2	4
Bureaucratic mediation	1.92	1.29	56	20	7	10	7
Reading	1.48	0.96	74	13	8	1	4
Career education	1.01	0.11	99	1	0	0	0
Enrichment	1.29	0.58	77	19	3	1	0
Protection	1.88	1.18	55	20	12	10	4
Total Child Help	27.55	8.83	—	—	—	—	—

tion (7%). It is clear from these low percentages that most of the adult children who do provide help to their parents provide only a low to moderate level of help. For example, in regard to help with parents' maintenance needs, 45% of adult children provided no help and 55% provided some degree of help. However, 25% gave only occasional help, 12% gave some regular help, 10% gave a great deal of help, and only 8% provided all or almost all of the parents' needs for maintenance. This same pattern was typical of responses in most service areas.

Means and standard deviations for the amount of services provided by adult children to their parents are also presented in Table 5-2. Means for the 16 types of services range from 1.01 to 2.73. The area in which the adult children provided the greatest amount of service to parents was psychological support (M = 2.73), followed by maintenance (M = 2.11), transportation (M = 2.03), bureaucratic mediation (M = 1.92), protection (M = 1.88), and homemaking (M = 1.79).

A factor analysis of the scores in the 16 service areas indicated a single general factor, as was the case with the parents' service needs.

The scores for the 16 types of service were summed to yield a total children's help score. The mean score was 27.55 (SD = 8.83), indicating an overall level of help from adult children to elderly parents which was only occasional.

Adult Children's Commitment to Provide Future Help

Since a large proportion of elderly parents needed little, if any, services from children or other service providers at the present time, the adult children were asked about the extent to which they could help their parents in a hypothetical future situation where the parents needed a great deal of help. The same five-point response scale which was used for present help to parents was also employed for future help. This commitment to provide future help to parents is summarized in Table 5-3.

Table 5-3   Amount of Anticipated Future Help Provided to Elderly Parents by Adult Children in 16 Service Areas: Group Means and Response Frequencies

			Percentage of Responses			
Type of Service	Mean	SD	None	Occa-sional help	Some reg. help	Great deal help	All or almost all
Homemaking	3.24	1.28	13	15	27	26	20
Housing	3.40	1.28	12	10	28	26	24
Income	3.14	1.02	7	15	44	25	9
Maintenance	3.10	1.28	15	16	27	26	15
Personal care	3.08	1.18	12	19	30	27	12
Home health care	3.04	1.20	12	21	29	26	12
Transportation	3.24	1.28	14	12	27	29	18
Psychological support	3.50	0.94	2	13	28	46	11
Social and recreation	2.80	1.14	15	24	32	21	7
Employment	1.58	1.14	75	5	11	3	5
Spiritual	3.01	1.28	19	13	26	32	10
Bureaucratic mediation	3.32	1.30	13	12	24	30	21
Reading	3.21	1.18	12	13	30	33	12
Career education	1.51	1.04	76	9	6	7	2
Enrichment	2.32	1.32	40	18	18	18	5
Protection	3.12	1.24	14	16	27	30	13
Total Future Child Help	45.52	11.80	—	—	—	—	—

The percentages of adult children who felt no future commitment to provide any degree of help to their parents in time of need ranged from 2% to 76%. The highest percentages of adult children with no commitment to help were found for career education (76%), employment (75%), enrichment (40%), and spiritual (19%) services. The high percentages for career education, employment, and enrichment services reflected not so much an unwillingness to help as a belief that such activities were preposterous for the elderly to undertake. Many of the interviewees just could not imagine their elderly parents as being interested in further work or personal growth at this stage in their lives.

The lowest percentages, indicating the fewest adult children with no commitment to help and, conversely, the largest numbers of children with some commitment for future help, were found for psychological support (2%) and income (7%). For housing, personal care, home health care, and reading materials services, 12% of adult children reported no future commitment; the figure was 13% for homemaking and bureaucratic mediation, 14% for transportation and protection, and 15% for maintenance and social and recreation services. One can conclude from these data that 85% or more of adult children feel some degree of commitment to provide help to their elderly parents in 12 of the 16 types of service considered.

At the other end of the response scale, the highest percentages of adult children who were willing to provide all or almost all of their parents' needs for services were found for housing (24%), bureaucratic mediation (21%), homemaking (20%), transportation (18%), and maintenance (15%). The lowest percentages (2% to 5%) were found for career education, employment, and enrichment. It is noteworthy that social and recreation services (7%) and income (9%) were also low, indicating that very few children wished to take full responsibility for their parents' needs in these areas.

Means and standard deviations for the amount of future help from adult children are also presented in Table 5-3. Means range from 1.51 to 3.50, with the greatest amount of future help to be expected in the areas of psychological support (M = 3.50), housing (M = 3.40), bureaucratic mediation (M = 3.32), homemaking (M = 3.24), and transportation (M = 3.24). Means for income, maintenance, personal care, home health care, spiritual, reading, and protection services were all between 3.01 and 3.21. For all these service areas, the average level of commitment to parents was for some regular help but less than a great deal of help. The least amount of future help can be expected in the areas of career education (M = 1.51), employment (M = 1.58), enrichment (M = 2.32), and social and recreation services (M = 2.80).

Again, a total score for future help from adult children was obtained by summing scores over the 16 service areas on the basis of factor analytic results. The mean of this total score was 45.52 (SD = 11.80), representing a level of help somewhat lower than some regular help. The total mean score for future help was more than one and one-half times as large as the mean for present child help, indicating that most adult children were willing to increase the amount of help to their elderly parents by a substantial amount if the occasion called for it. However, most of the adult children felt committed only to the provision of intermediate levels of service to their parents; only a small minority were willing to assume the entire burden of services to parents in any area.

Children's Help in Relation to Parents' Needs

To explore the question of whether children gave help to their elderly parents in proportion to their perceptions of the degree of parental need for services, Pearson product moment correlations were computed between the scores for the parents' present needs for service, present help from children, and commitment to provide help in the future. The correlation between parents' need for services (as perceived by the adult children) and the amount of services provided by the adult children is 0.78 ($p < .01$). This indicates that adult children are providing services to parents when they recognize their parents' need for help; those who see a greater need are also the ones who give a greater amount of help. When correlations were computed for each of the 16 types of service, correlations ranging from .57 to .72 were obtained for all services except career education ($r = .49$) and employment ($r = .20$).

The correlation between parents' present need for services and the adult children's commitment to help in the future is 0.18 ($p = .02$), indicating only a weak relationship. This is not unexpected in view of the fact that most parents have low needs for services at the present time. Correlations for each of the 16 types of service were also low, and were statistically significant only for housing, maintenance, transportation, psychological support, social and recreational activities, spiritual, bureaucratic mediation, reading materials, enrichment, and protection services.

Finally, the correlation between present services to parents from adult children and the children's commitment to provide future services in time of need was 0.52 ($p < .01$). The correlations were significant for all types of service except career education, and were above .30 for all areas except income, employment, personal care, and home health care services. These correlations suggest that the adult children who are most likely to provide larger amounts of help in the future are those who are now providing the most help.

Children's Ability to Help and Importance of Service Type

As an additional means of examining the congruence between parents' needs for services and children's helping behavior, the study participants were asked to rank the 16 service areas, first by the relative importance of parental need, and second by the children's ability to provide help. The mean rankings are presented in Table 5-4. Service areas in descending order of parental need (as judged by the adult child) are: transportation, homemaking, maintenance, personal care, home health care, psychological support, protection, and social and recreation activities. Service areas in descending order of

Table 5-4　The 16 Service Areas Ranked in Order of Parents' Needs for Services and Adult Children's Ability to Provide Services (Mean Ranks)

Type of Service	Parents' Needs		Children's Ability	
	Mean	SD	Mean	SD
Homemaking	5.59	4.01	5.44	3.62
Housing	8.23	4.88	6.61	4.54
Income	8.68	4.88	8.27	4.69
Maintenance	5.71	3.69	6.20	3.54
Personal care	5.94	3.60	6.08	3.73
Home health care	5.97	3.60	6.96	3.60
Transportation	5.39	3.62	6.05	3.74
Psychological support	6.30	3.79	4.97	3.72
Social and recreation	7.98	3.84	8.84	3.34
Employment	13.87	3.25	14.35	2.54
Spiritual	8.58	3.66	8.62	4.00
Bureaucratic mediation	8.12	3.83	7.99	4.28
Reading	9.88	3.36	9.07	3.48
Career education	14.20	2.59	14.36	2.16
Enrichment	11.80	3.56	12.62	2.94
Protection	7.79	3.73	9.10	3.70

adult children's ability to provide services are: psychological support, homemaking, transportation, personal care, maintenance, housing, home health care, and bureaucratic mediation. Thus while there are some differences in the top eight group of services when ranked in the two ways, there does exist a general correspondence between the two sets of ranks. This was borne out by a rank-order correlation of .84 between the importance of area of parental need and adult children's ability to help.

Services Provided by Adult Children's Siblings

The amount of help provided by the siblings of the adult children to the elderly parents of the adult children who were interviewed is presented in Table 5-5. These data are presented for the 145 adult children who had living siblings.

The percentages of interviewees reporting *no* help from siblings to their parents ranged from 29% to 99%. The largest percentages of

Table 5-5   Amount of Help Provided by Adult Children's Siblings to Elderly Parents in 16 Service Areas: Group Means and Response Frequencies

			Percentage of Responses				
Type of Service	Mean	SD	None	Occa-sional help	Some reg. help	Great deal help	All or almost all
Homemaking	1.68	0.91	61	24	10	4	1
Housing	1.11	0.46	95	2	3	1	0
Income	1.11	0.39	92	5	2	0	0
Maintenance	1.81	1.02	57	21	15	5	1
Personal care	1.16	0.45	89	8	3	0	0
Home health care	1.17	0.50	90	7	3	1	0
Transportation	1.77	1.17	66	15	8	7	4
Psychological support	2.41	0.98	29	29	28	13	0
Social and recreation	1.40	0.71	75	16	8	1	0
Employment	1.01	0.08	99	1	0	0	0
Spiritual	1.27	0.64	83	13	2	2	0
Bureaucratic mediation	1.81	1.22	66	11	12	5	5
Reading	1.26	0.64	85	10	4	1	1
Career education	1.01	0.08	99	1	0	0	0
Enrichment	1.26	0.59	82	14	3	1	0
Protection	1.58	0.89	67	19	9	5	0
Total Sibling Help	22.79	5.84	—	—	—	—	—

Note: Means and standard deviations were computed for 145 interviewees with living siblings.

siblings providing no help were found for employment (99%), career education (99%), housing (95%), income (92%), home health care (90%), and personal care (89%). The lowest percentages, indicating areas where there were fewer siblings providing no help to parents, were found for psychological support (29%), maintenance (57%), homemaking (61%), transportation (66%), and bureaucratic mediation (66%).

Looking at the other end of the response scale, the percentages pertaining to siblings who provide all or almost all of the parents' needs for service ranged from 0 to 5%. The highest percentages were found for bureaucratic mediation (5%), transportation (4%), homemaking (1%), maintenance (1%), and reading (1%). For the remainder of the service areas, no interviewees reported any siblings who provided all or almost all of their parents' service needs.

Means and standard deviations for the amount of help provided by the siblings of the 145 study participants with living siblings are also presented in Table 5-5. The greatest amount of sibling help was provided in the area of psychological support (M = 2.41), followed by maintenance (M = 1.80), bureaucratic mediation (M = 1.81), transportation (M = 1.77), homemaking (M = 1.68), protection (M = 1.58), and social and recreation (M = 1.40). These means represent less than occasional help, except for psychological support which was given at a level somewhat greater than occasional help.

Areas where the least amount of sibling help was reported were employment (M = 1.01), career education (M = 1.01), housing (M = 1.11), income (M = 1.11), personal care (M = 1.16), and home health care (M = 1.17). These means represent a level of help which is only slightly greater than no help at all.

When the scores were summed over the 16 types of service to yield a total sibling help score, the mean was 22.79 (SD = 5.84). Overall, the mean level of help was less than occasional help to parents. In comparison to the mean of 27.55 obtained for help from the adult children who participated in the study, the help reported for siblings was lower. The difference was not great however.

The adult children were also asked to indicate which sibling provided the most help to their parents in each of the service areas. There were differences in the frequencies of naming brothers and sisters. Areas in which a brother was named more frequently were maintenance, bureaucratic mediation, and protection. Areas in which a sister was named more frequently were homemaking, personal care, home health care, transportation, psychological support, and social and recreation services. In the remaining areas (housing, income, employment, enrichment, career education, and reading materials), brothers and sisters were named to about the same degree.

Future Sibling Help

Study participants were asked about the amount of help which their parents could anticipate from their siblings at some time in the future when the parents would need a great deal more help. They were asked first about help from brothers and then about help from sisters.

There were 99 study participants with living brothers. The amount of anticipated help from brothers is summarized in Table 5-6. The percentage of adult children expecting *no* future help from

Table 5-6   Amount of Anticipated Future Help Provided to Elderly Parents by Brothers of Adult Children in 16 Service Areas: Group Means and Response Frequencies

| | | | *Percentage of Responses* | | | |
Type of Service	Mean	SD	None	Occa-sional help	Some reg. help	Great deal help	All or almost all
Homemaking	2.54	1.17	55	12	18	12	2
Housing	2.73	1.20	54	7	21	15	2
Income	2.87	0.99	48	9	29	14	1
Maintenance	2.80	1.20	53	8	19	18	2
Personal care	2.35	1.04	56	15	21	7	1
Home health care	2.32	1.11	58	15	17	9	1
Transportation	2.57	1.19	55	11	20	12	2
Psychological support	2.97	1.03	46	13	18	21	1
Social and recreation	2.33	1.02	55	18	19	7	1
Employment	1.37	0.81	86	6	5	1	1
Spiritual	2.48	1.19	58	10	18	13	1
Bureaucratic mediation	2.66	1.35	58	9	14	15	5
Reading	2.49	1.09	54	15	20	10	1
Career education	1.38	0.84	87	5	5	2	1
Enrichment	1.91	1.08	70	12	12	5	1
Protection	2.69	1.13	51	13	20	13	2
Total Future Help from Brothers	38.52	11.66	—	—	—	—	—

Note: Means and standard deviations were computed for 99 interviewees with living brothers.

brothers to their aging parents ranged from 46% to 87%. However, these percentages varied in a narrower range from 46% to 58%, with the exception of employment (86%), career education (87%), and enrichment (70%). By contrast, the percentages of adult children who felt that brothers would provide all or almost all of their elderly parents' future service needs ranged from 1% to 5%. The highest percentages were found for bureaucratic mediation (5%), and for homemaking, housing, maintenance, transportation, and protection (all at 2%); for the remainder of the 16 service areas, it was 1%.

The mean scores for future service from brothers also varied within a rather narrow range, with the exception of employment, career education, and enrichment. Highest means were found for psychological support (M = 2.97), income (M = 2.87), and maintenance (M = 2.80). This represents a level below that of some regular help.

A total score for future help from brothers was obtained by summing over the 16 service areas. This mean was 38.52 (SD = 11.66).

Similarly, the 102 adult children with living sisters were asked about the amount of future help from sisters to elderly parents. The amount of expected help is summarized in Table 5-7. The percentage of adult children expecting *no* future help to their parents from sisters ranged from 43% to 87% (almost identical to the range for brothers). As was the case for brothers, the percentages varied in a narrow range with the exception of career education (87%), employment (85%), and enrichment (66%). At the other end of the response scale, the percentages of adult children who felt that sisters would provide all or almost all of their parents' future service needs ranged from 1% to 4%. The highest percentages were found for transportation (4%) and for homemaking, housing, psychological support and bureaucratic mediation (all at 3%); the percentage for the remainder of the 16 types of service was 1%.

Means ranged from 1.40 to 3.11. However, with the exception of career education, employment, and enrichment, the means varied within a relatively narrow range. The highest means were found for psychological support (M = 3.11), income (M = 2.79), homemaking (M = 2.77), housing (M = 2.74), and protection (M = 2.74). These means indicated a level of expected future help to parents which was at or somewhat below the level of some regular help.

A total score for future help from sisters was obtained by summing over the 16 types of service. The mean was 39.33 (SD = 11.60). This was only a little higher than the mean for future help from brothers.

Table 5-7 Amount of Anticipated Future Help Provided to Elderly Parents by Sisters of Adult Children in 16 Service Areas: Group Means and Response Frequencies

Type of Service	Mean	SD	None	Occa-sional help	Some reg. help	Great deal help	All or almost all
					Percentage of Responses		
Homemaking	2.77	1.11	48	14	22	13	3
Housing	2.74	1.16	51	9	24	13	3
Income	2.79	0.94	46	10	33	10	1
Maintenance	2.42	1.08	55	13	22	10	1
Personal care	2.64	1.13	52	10	23	14	1
Home health care	2.53	1.16	54	12	19	13	1
Transportation	2.53	1.30	57	11	15	13	4
Psychological support	3.11	1.05	43	12	19	23	3
Social and recreation	2.49	1.11	52	16	18	12	1
Employment	1.45	0.91	85	5	7	2	1
Spiritual	2.47	1.15	55	11	20	13	1
Bureaucratic mediation	2.63	1.26	54	12	15	16	3
Reading	2.64	1.07	49	16	20	13	1
Career education	1.40	0.88	87	6	4	3	1
Enrichment	1.99	1.11	66	15	10	8	1
Protection	2.74	1.13	49	14	17	18	1
Total Future Help from Sisters	39.33	11.60	—	—	—	—	—

Note: Means and standard deviations were computed for 102 interviewees with living sisters.

These data suggest that future help to parents is expected from both brothers and sisters at roughly the same levels, with neither expected to take over the entire burden of parent care. The emphasis of the help seems to depend to a degree on the sex of the sibling. For example, brothers are regarded as more likely to provide future help with parents' maintenance needs (a traditional male role), while sisters are more likely to provide future help in such traditionally feminine areas as homemaking, personal care, and home health care.

Present Help from Other Kin

The adult children of the elderly were also asked about the amount of help which elderly parents received from other members of the kin network, such as the parents' siblings, cousins, nieces, nephews, grandchildren, and so on. Also included were the parents' relatives through marriage, such as brothers- or sisters-in-law and other spouses of consanguineous kin. The amount of help is summarized in Table 5-8. The percentage reporting that their parents received *no* help from kin other than their children varied from 61% to 100%. The lowest percentages (indicating the fewest adult children reporting no help to parents from kin, and, conversely, the greatest amount of kin help) were found for psychological support (61%), social and recreation (85%), maintenance (86%), homemaking (87%), transportation (88%), and protection (88%). At the other end of the response scale, the percentage of adult children who reported that other kin provided all or almost all of elderly parents' service needs was 0% for all types of service except maintenance (1%) and transportation (1%).

Means were similarly low, ranging from 1.00 to 1.57. The highest mean amounts of kin help were found for psychological support (M = 1.57), maintenance (M = 1.26), homemaking (M = 1.22), social and recreational activities (M = 1.19), and transportation (M = 1.18). These means represent a level of help which is either nonexistent or quite rare.

Table 5-8   Amount of Help Provided to Elderly Parents by Other Kin in 16
Service Areas: Group Means and Response Frequencies

| | | | Percentage of Responses | | | |
| | | | None | Occa-sional help | Some reg. help | Great deal help | All or almost all |
Type of Service	Mean	SD	None				
Homemaking	1.22	0.62	87	7	5	2	0
Housing	1.02	0.22	99	0	1	0	0
Income	1.00	0.00	100	0	0	0	0
Maintenance	1.26	0.72	86	6	5	2	1
Personal care	1.04	0.29	98	1	1	1	0
Home health care	1.04	0.32	98	0	1	1	0
Transportation	1.18	0.57	88	8	3	1	1
Psychological support	1.57	0.81	61	23	15	2	0
Social and recreation	1.19	0.51	85	12	2	1	0
Employment	1.00	0.00	100	0	0	0	0
Spiritual	1.10	0.32	91	9	1	0	0
Bureaucratic mediation	1.09	0.40	94	4	2	1	0
Reading	1.10	0.40	93	4	2	1	0
Career education	1.00	0.00	100	0	0	0	0
Enrichment	1.06	0.28	96	3	1	0	0
Protection	1.16	0.48	88	8	3	1	0
Total Help from Other Kin	18.02	2.78	—	—	—	—	—

Table 5-9 Percentages of Adult Children of Elderly Parents Naming Other Kin as Service Providers in 16 Service Areas

	Type of Elderly Parents' Kin					
Type of Service	*Sibling*	*Cousin*	*Niece/ nephew*	*Grand-child*	*In-laws*	*Other kin*
Homemaking	3	0	2	6	2	0
Housing	1	0	0	1	0	0
Income	0	0	0	0	0	0
Maintenance	1	0	1	7	5	1
Personal care	0	0	0	1	1	0
Home health care	0	0	0	1	1	0
Transportation	2	0	2	6	1	0
Psychological support	21	3	2	5	5	2
Social and recreation	7	2	1	2	1	1
Employment	0	0	0	0	0	0
Spiritual	2	0	1	5	1	1
Bureaucratic mediation	2	1	1	1	2	0
Reading	2	1	0	1	1	0
Career education	0	0	0	0	0	0
Enrichment	2	1	0	1	1	0
Protection	4	0	1	4	1	1

The amount of kin help was summed over the 16 service areas to yield a total kin help score. The mean was 18.02 (SD = 2.78), which indicated a considerably lower amount of help from other kin than from the study participants themselves or from their siblings.

To determine which kin members were providing help, even to a limited degree, the adult child was asked to specify which kin members provided help to elderly parents when such help was given. This information was coded into six categories of kin according to their relationship to the interviewee's elderly parents: siblings, cousins, nieces and nephews, grandchildren, "in-laws" and "other kin" (which included parents, aunts and uncles, and more distant kin). The percentages of kin in each of these categories are presented in Table 5-9. Examining the table, it is apparent that the elderly parents' siblings and grandchildren were most frequently named as service providers, followed by kin through marriage. In the area of psychological support, siblings were named by 21%, grandchildren by 5%, and in-laws by 5%. In the area of social and recreation needs, siblings were named by 7%, grandchildren by 2%, and cousins by 2%. In the area of protection, siblings and grandchildren were each named by 4%. However, in the areas of homemaking, maintenance, transportation, and spiritual needs, grandchildren were named more frequently (5% to 7%) than were siblings. The grandchildren's role thus appears to be greater in areas which require the execution of physical tasks, while the siblings' role appears to be stronger in social and intangible psychological areas.

Future Services from Other Kin

Adult children of the elderly were asked about the extent to which their parents could expect help in time of future need from other members of the kin network. Their expectation of future help from kin other than themselves and their brothers and sisters is summarized in Table 5-10. Percentages of adult children who expect *no* future help for their parents from other kin ranged from 58% to 96%. The highest percentages, indicating the least potential help, were found for career education (96%), employment (95%), and income (90%). The lowest percentages, indicating the greatest amount of

Table 5-10 Amount of Anticipated Future Help Provided to Elderly Parents by Other Kin in 16 Service Areas: Group Means and Response Frequencies

			Percentage of Responses				
Type of Service	Mean	SD	None	Occa-sional help	Some reg. help	Great deal help	All or almost all
Homemaking	1.49	0.91	72	13	10	4	1
Housing	1.20	0.61	88	5	5	2	0
Income	1.18	0.61	90	4	4	2	0
Maintenance	1.40	0.87	79	8	7	5	1
Personal care	1.29	0.71	81	12	4	2	1
Home health care	1.30	0.73	81	11	5	2	1
Transportation	1.44	0.80	70	21	7	2	1
Psychological support	1.74	1.04	58	20	13	8	1
Social and recreation	1.48	0.80	69	18	10	3	0
Employment	1.08	0.37	95	4	1	1	0
Spiritual	1.40	0.76	74	15	8	3	0
Bureaucratic mediation	1.29	0.72	83	8	6	3	0
Reading	1.47	0.86	72	15	8	5	0
Career education	1.05	0.27	96	2	1	0	0
Enrichment	1.38	0.79	76	14	5	5	0
Protection	1.40	0.80	75	15	5	0	0
Total Future Help from Other Kin	21.60	7.56	—	—	—	—	—

potential help, were in the areas of psychological support (58%), social and recreational activities (69%), and transportation services (70%). Only 1% expected other kin to provide all or almost all of the elderly parents' needs for services in the areas of homemaking, maintenance, personal care, home health care, transportation, and psychological support; for all other areas it was 0%.

Means and standard deviations for the amount of future help anticipated from other kin are also presented in Table 5-10. The greatest amount of future help can be expected in the areas of psychological support (M = 1.74), homemaking (M = 1.49), social and recreation (M = 1.48), and reading materials services (M = 1.47). The least amount of future help can be expected in the areas of career education (M = 1.05) and employment (M = 1.08). Thus, the level of expected future help from kin is at best below the level of occasional help, and is almost nonexistent in other areas.

A total score for future help from other kin was obtained by summing over the 16 service areas. The mean score was 21.60 (SD = 7.56). This represents only a modest increase in the amount of kin help anticipated in the future when compared to the help which elderly parents receive at present from these other kin.

As with present help, the adult children were asked to name the members of the kin network who were expected to provide help in the future. Responses were coded into the same six categories.

The percentages of kin in each of the six categories who were named by adult children as expected to provide future help to elderly parents are presented in Table 5-11. As with present help from other kin, the elderly parents' siblings and grandchildren were the most frequently named service providers, followed by kin through marriage. Siblings were named more frequently than grandchildren in most service areas, with grandchildren named more frequently only for maintenance and transportation services. Areas in which siblings were named most often were psychological support (21%), social and recreational activities (15%), spiritual (12%), reading materials (11%), homemaking (10%), and enrichment (10%). Grandchildren were most frequently named in the areas of transportation (12%), psychological support (10%), homemaking (10%), and maintenance (9%). Interestingly, in-laws were named with a frequency of 9% in the area of maintenance help, suggesting that the spouse of a kin member may be expected to provide help with types of maintenance where special skills are required.

Table 5-11 **Percentages of Adult Children of Elderly Parents Naming Other Kin as Anticipated Providers of Future Help to Parents in 16 Service Areas**

Type of Service	Type of Elderly Parents' Kin					
	Sibling	Cousin	Niece/ nephew	Grand- child	In-laws	Other kin
Homemaking	10	1	3	10	4	0
Housing	6	0	1	3	1	1
Income	5	1	0	2	0	2
Maintenance	4	1	1	9	9	1
Personal care	7	0	1	6	5	1
Home health care	7	0	1	7	2	1
Transportation	9	0	3	12	5	1
Psychological support	21	2	2	10	5	1
Social and recreation	15	1	2	6	4	2
Employment	2	0	1	2	1	0
Spiritual	12	0	2	7	2	1
Bureaucratic mediation	6	0	1	4	4	1
Reading	11	1	1	7	4	1
Career education	2	0	0	1	1	0
Enrichment	10	1	2	4	4	0
Protection	7	0	4	7	4	1

Kin Help in Relation to Parents' Needs

When correlations were computed between the amount of present and future services from other kin and the elderly parents' needs for help, need was significantly but weakly correlated ($r = .22$) with present help from other kin, but not with expected future help. Present help from other kin was correlated substantially ($r = .66$) with future help. The amount of help presently given to parents by adult children was also significantly but weakly correlated with the amount of present help from other kin ($r = .22$), but not with expected future help. One can conclude that where elderly parents have a need for help and where adult children are helping those parents, other kin also have a tendency to help. Those members of the kin network who are presently providing services to elderly parents of the study participants are expected to provide more help in the future.

Future Services from Government Agencies

Adult children of elderly parents were also asked about the services which they anticipated from various nonfamily service providers at some future time when their parents would need a great deal of help. The first type of provider considered was government agencies.

The amount of future help expected from government sources is summarized in Table 5-12. The percentage of adult children who expected their elderly parents to get *no* government help ranged from 27% to 87%. The highest percentages of adult children expecting no government help were found for spiritual (87%), career education (85%), and employment (84%), followed most closely by enrichment services (68%). The lowest percentages, indicating the smallest frequency of those expecting no government help or, conversely, the largest amount of help, were found for income (27%),

Table 5-12 **Amount of Anticipated Future Help Provided to Elderly Parents by Government Agencies in 16 Service Areas: Group Means and Response Frequencies**

| | | | | Percentage of Responses | | | |
| | | | | | | | |
Type of Service	Mean	SD	None	Occa-sional help	Some reg. help	Great deal help	All or almost all
Homemaking	1.73	0.93	56	19	22	2	1
Housing	1.77	1.01	54	23	16	4	2
Income	2.43	1.06	27	16	45	9	2
Maintenance	1.57	0.83	62	23	13	2	1
Personal care	1.61	0.83	58	26	13	2	1
Home health care	1.93	0.91	41	29	27	2	1
Transportation	1.74	0.89	50	30	17	2	1
Psychological support	1.49	0.76	65	24	9	1	1
Social and recreation	1.57	0.89	65	20	11	4	1
Employment	1.24	0.62	84	10	6	0	1
Spiritual	1.16	0.50	87	10	2	0	1
Bureaucratic mediation	1.61	0.82	57	27	13	2	1
Reading	1.60	0.84	60	24	14	2	1
Career education	1.24	0.68	85	10	3	0	2
Enrichment	1.51	0.85	68	18	11	3	1
Protection	1.78	0.97	52	25	18	3	2
Total Future Government Help	25.97	7.99	—	—	—	—	—

home health care (41%), transportation (50%), protection (52%), and housing (54%).

Looking at the other end of the response scale, only very small percentages of adult children (1% to 2%) expected their parents to get government help for all or almost all of their service needs. In only one area, income, did an appreciable percentage (9%) expect their parents to get a great deal of government help.

Means and standard deviations for the amount of expected government help are also presented in Table 5-12. The greatest amounts of future government help were found for income ($M = 2.43$), home health care ($M = 1.93$), protection ($M = 1.78$), housing ($M = 1.77$), transportation ($M = 1.74$), and homemaking ($M = 1.73$). The least amount of government services was anticipated in areas of spiritual ($M = 1.16$), career education ($M = 1.24$), and employment services ($M = 1.24$).

A total score for future government services was obtained by summing over the 16 service areas. The mean score was 25.97 ($SD = 7.99$). This is somewhat more than expected from other kin, but a great deal less than adult children themselves are committed to provide in the future.

Future Help from Voluntary Organizations

The amount of help expected from voluntary organizations in the future is summarized in Table 5-13. The percentage of adult children who expected *no* future help for their parents from voluntary organizations ranged from 27% to 86%. The highest percentages were found for career education (86%), employment (82%), and housing (70%). The lowest percentages, indicating the most future services, were found for spiritual (27%), transportation (39%), home health care (41%), and reading materials (41%) services.

Looking at the other end of the response scale, only for four service areas (transportation, bureaucratic mediation, enrichment, and protection) do as many as 1% of adult children expect all or almost all of their parents' needs to be provided by voluntary organizations. In fact, only in the spiritual area did as many as 9% anticipate a great deal of help.

Means and standard deviations for the amount of expected future help from voluntary organizations are also presented in Table 5-13. The greatest amounts of future help from voluntary organizations

Table 5-13   **Amount of Anticipated Future Help Provided to Elderly Parents by Voluntary Organizations in 16 Service Areas: Group Means and Response Frequencies**

Type of Service	Mean	SD	None	Occasional help	Some reg. help	Great deal help	All or almost all
				Percentage of Responses			
Homemaking	1.66	0.71	48	40	12	1	0
Housing	1.37	0.62	70	23	7	0	0
Income	1.46	0.69	65	26	9	1	0
Maintenance	1.51	0.69	59	31	9	1	0
Personal care	1.67	0.72	46	41	11	1	0
Home health care	1.81	0.79	41	37	21	1	0
Transportation	1.82	0.80	39	42	17	1	1
Psychological support	1.63	0.75	51	37	9	2	0
Social and recreation	1.79	0.90	48	31	16	5	0
Employment	1.23	0.54	82	13	4	1	0
Spiritual	2.23	1.04	27	38	22	10	0
Bureaucratic mediation	1.48	0.72	64	26	10	0	1
Reading	1.82	0.82	41	39	17	3	0
Career education	1.18	0.50	86	10	3	1	0
Enrichment	1.67	0.87	54	30	12	4	1
Protection	1.73	0.85	49	33	15	2	1
Total Future Help from Voluntary Organizations	26.06	6.95	—	—	—	—	—

were found for spiritual ($M = 2.23$), transportation ($M = 1.82$), reading materials ($M = 1.82$), home health care ($M = 1.81$), and social and recreation services ($M = 1.79$). The least amount of future help was expected for career education ($M = 1.18$) and employment services ($M = 1.23$).

A total score for future help from voluntary organizations was obtained by summing over the 16 types of service. The mean score was 26.06 (SD = 6.95), about the same as for government help.

Future Help from Friends

The amount of help anticipated for elderly parents from friends is summarized in Table 5-14. The percentage of adult children who expected *no* future help for their parents from friends ranged from 32% to 91%. The highest percentages, indicating the least help from friends, were found for career education (91%), employment (86%), and income (81%). The lowest percentages, indicating the most help, were found for psychological support (32%), social and recreation (34%), transportation (38%), spiritual (40%), and reading materials services (40%). Looking at the other end of the response scale, only 1% of adult children expected parents to get all or almost all of their service needs from friends in the areas of income and personal care; in all other service areas the percentage was zero.

Means and standard deviations for the amount of anticipated help from friends are also presented in Table 5-14. The greatest amounts of help were found for psychological support ($M = 1.92$), social and recreation ($M = 1.92$), spiritual ($M = 1.84$), homemaking ($M = 1.80$), reading ($M = 1.78$), transportation ($M = 1.79$), and protection ($M = 1.76$). The least amounts of help were found for career education ($M = 1.10$), employment ($M = 1.20$), and income ($M = 1.23$). These means indicate a level of future help from friends which is below the level of occasional help.

Table 5-14 Amount of Anticipated Future Help Provided to Elderly Parents by Friends in 16 Service Areas: Group Means and Response Frequencies

| | | | | Percentage of Responses | | | |
Type of Service	Mean	SD	None	Occa-sional help	Some reg. help	Great deal help	All or almost all
Homemaking	1.80	0.82	41	43	12	4	0
Housing	1.32	0.61	74	20	5	1	0
Income	1.23	0.51	81	16	2	1	1
Maintenance	1.53	0.67	55	37	6	1	0
Personal care	1.43	0.65	63	31	5	0	1
Home health care	1.48	0.63	59	35	5	1	0
Transportation	1.79	0.73	38	48	13	2	0
Psychological support	1.92	0.80	32	48	15	4	0
Social and recreation	1.92	0.83	34	44	18	4	0
Employment	1.20	0.56	86	9	4	1	0
Spiritual	1.84	0.85	40	40	15	5	0
Bureaucratic mediation	1.27	0.56	77	20	2	1	0
Reading	1.78	0.77	40	46	12	3	0
Career education	1.10	0.34	91	7	1	0	0
Enrichment	1.55	0.68	55	36	9	1	0
Protection	1.76	0.78	42	43	12	3	0
Total Future Help from Friends	24.91	6.89	—	—	—	—	—

A total score for future help from friends was obtained by summing over the 16 service areas. The mean score was 24.91 (SD = 6.89), slightly less than for help from government agencies or voluntary organizations.

Future Help from Neighbors

The adult children were also asked about the amount of future help to be expected for their elderly parents from neighbors. These data are summarized in Table 5-15.

The percentage of adult children who expected their parents to receive *no* help from neighbors ranged from 40% to 94%. The highest percentages, indicating the least amount of help, were found for career education (94%), employment (88%), and income (86%). The lowest percentages, indicating the most help, were found for protection (40%), homemaking (42%), transportation (46%), psychological support (48%), and social and recreation services (51%).

Table 5-15   Amount of Anticipated Future Help Provided to Elderly Parents by Neighbors in 16 Service Areas: Group Means and Response Frequencies

| | | | | *Percentage of Responses* | | | |
| | | | | | | | |
Type of Service	Mean	SD	None	Occasional help	Some reg. help	Great deal help	All or almost all
Homemaking	1.74	0.77	42	46	7	4	0
Housing	1.25	0.55	80	16	4	1	0
Income	1.16	0.45	86	12	1	1	0
Maintenance	1.55	0.68	54	38	7	1	0
Personal care	1.37	0.63	70	26	4	0	1
Home health care	1.38	0.59	67	29	4	1	0
Transportation	1.63	0.67	46	45	7	1	0
Psychological support	1.65	0.75	48	41	7	3	0
Social and recreation	1.62	0.71	51	38	10	1	0
Employment	1.16	0.51	88	8	2	1	0
Spiritual	1.55	0.73	57	32	9	2	0
Bureaucratic mediation	1.18	0.43	84	15	3	0	0
Reading	1.61	0.75	52	37	9	2	0
Career education	1.07	0.27	94	5	1	0	0
Enrichment	1.35	0.57	70	27	3	1	0
Protection	1.78	0.81	40	48	8	3	1
Total Future Help from Neighbors	23.05	6.51	—	—	—	—	—

At the other end of the response scale, only a small percentage of adult children expected neighbors to provide all or almost all of their parents' service needs. This was in the areas of personal care (1%) and income (1%); in all other areas the percentage was zero.

Means and standard deviations for the amount of anticipated help from neighbors are also presented in Table 5-15. The greatest amounts of future help from neighbors were found for protection (M = 1.78), homemaking (M = 1.74), psychological support (M = 1.65), transportation (M = 1.63), and social and recreation (M = 1.62) services. The smallest amounts of help were found for career education (M = 1.07), employment (M = 1.16), and income (M = 1.16).

A total score for future help from neighbors was obtained by summing over the 16 types of service. The mean score was 23.05 (SD = 6.51), less than the mean for future help from friends. Overall, this represents a level of help that is somewhat less than occasional help.

Future Services from Hired Providers

The final nonfamily service provider which was to be considered in the study was the hired provider. The study participants were asked how much future services they expected their parents to receive from hired sources of help. The amount of future help from hired providers is summarized in Table 5-16. The table does not include income, as this service area is not meaningful in this context.

The percentages of adult children who expect *no* future help from hired providers ranged from 27% to 94%. The highest percentages, indicating the least use of hired help, were found for career education (94%), employment (93%), and spiritual services (91%). The lowest percentages, indicating the greatest use of hired service providers, were found for home health care (27%), maintenance (37%), homemaking (38%) and personal care (38%).

At the other end of the response scale, the percentage of adult children who responded that their parents would hire all or almost all needed services ranged from 0% to 6%. The highest percentages were found for homemaking (6%), home health care (5%), maintenance (4%), and personal care (4%).

Means and standard deviations for the amount of future help from hired providers are also presented in Table 5-16. The greatest amounts of hired help were found for home health care (M = 2.30), maintenance (M = 2.07), homemaking (M = 2.04), and personal

Table 5-16   Amount of Anticipated Future Help to Elderly Parents from Hired Providers in 15 Service Areas: Group Means and Response Frequencies

Type of Service	Mean	SD	Percentage of Responses				
			None	Occasional help	Some reg. help	Great deal help	All or almost all
Homemaking	2.04	1.13	38	35	16	4	6
Housing	1.67	1.04	62	21	10	5	3
Maintenance	2.07	1.09	37	34	18	7	4
Personal care	2.04	1.10	38	34	16	7	4
Home health care	2.30	1.12	27	37	22	9	5
Transportation	1.70	0.92	51	33	10	4	2
Psychological support	1.44	0.76	70	20	7	3	0
Social and recreation	1.21	0.51	84	13	3	1	0
Employment	1.12	0.46	93	4	2	1	0
Spiritual	1.10	0.36	91	7	2	0	0
Bureaucratic mediation	1.69	1.00	57	26	10	4	3
Reading	1.18	0.53	87	9	3	1	0
Career education	1.12	0.52	94	2	2	2	0
Enrichment	1.18	0.53	87	10	1	2	0
Protection	1.49	0.94	72	15	9	1	3
Total Future Hired Help	23.43	7.18	—	—	—	—	—

care ($M = 2.04$). These means represent slightly more than occasional hired help. The least amount of service from hired providers was anticipated for the areas of spiritual ($M = 1.10$), employment ($M = 1.12$), and career education services ($M = 1.12$).

A total score for future help from hired providers was obtained by summing over the 15 types of service. The mean score was 23.43 ($SD = 7.18$). Since only 15 types of service are involved, the score is not directly comparable with those for other providers.

Intercorrelations

To investigate the degree to which help from one provider was related to the help forthcoming from other providers, the intercorrelations between the total scores for elderly parents' service needs and present and future help from adult children, their siblings, extended kin, and other providers were computed. The matrix of these intercorrelations is presented in Table 5-17. In the interest of

Table 5-17   Intercorrelations of Total Scores for Parents' Service Needs and Help from Adult Children and Other Providers at Present and Expected in the Future

Score	1	2	3	4	5	6	7	8	9	10	11	12	13
1. Parents' needs	1.00	.78	.35	.22	.18	-.18	—	—	—	—	-.35	-.30	—
2. Adult children help		1.00	.21	.22	.52	-.16	—	—	—	—	-.17	-.17	-.21
3. Sibling help			1.00	.19	—	.34	.36	—	—	—	—	—	—
4. Other kin help				1.00	—	—	—	.66	—	—	—	—	—
5. Future children help					1.00	—	—	—	—	—	—	—	—
6. Future brothers' help						1.00	—	—	—	—	—	.16	—
7. Future sisters' help							1.00	—	—	—	—	.19	—
8. Future other kin help								1.00	—	.19	.19	.22	—
9. Future government help									1.00	.64	.32	.21	.27
10. Future help volunteer org.										1.00	.48	.41	.20
11. Future help friends											1.00	.75	.19
12. Future help neighbors												1.00	—
13. Future hired help													1.00

Note: Only correlations significant at the .05 level or less are included in the table.

clarity, only those correlations significant at the .05 level are included in the table.

It can be observed that elderly parents' present needs for service and the amounts of help from the adult children interviewed, their siblings, and other kin are positively related. That is, in those families where elderly parents have greater needs for service, adult children, their siblings, and other kin *all* tend to respond. The hypothesis that one member of a family acts to substitute for another who is missing or unable to assume a caretaking role is not supported by these data.

In response to parents' future needs, help from other kin, government, voluntary organizations, friends, neighbors, and hired providers are all positively interrelated. That is, adult children who expect their elderly parents to obtain help from one of these providers tend to expect them to obtain help from other providers as well. However, the help which adult children themselves expect to provide in the future is unrelated to their expectations of help in the future from other kin, government agencies, and voluntary organizations and is negatively related to help from friends, neighbors, and hired providers. That is, adult children who provide more service to their parents now tend to expect less future help from friends, neighbors, and hired providers.

Summary

The great majority of adult children see their elderly parents as having either very low needs or no needs for help from their children or other service providers. Adult children view their parents as having the greatest needs for services in the areas of maintenance, psychological support, transportation, bureaucratic mediation, homemaking, and protection. Transportation was the area in which the greatest percentage of parents (23%) depended completely on others for their needs.

These same areas were the ones in which the adult children provided the most help; overall, perceived parental need and amount of service from adult children were highly correlated ($r = .78$). Thus, adult children appear to be responsive to parental needs which they perceive.

Most adult children felt a considerable commitment to help their parents in the future if more help were to be needed. (For most service areas, only 12–15% indicated *no* commitment to help in the future.) Those giving more help now also expressed a greater commitment to help in the future $(r = .52)$. However, only a minority felt committed to provide all or almost all of their parents' needs.

In general, adult children viewed their siblings as providing somewhat less help to parents, now and in the future, than they themselves provided. Brothers and sisters are expected to help in areas consistent with traditional sex roles.

Areas in which the greatest help was received from other kin in the extended family were: psychological support, social and recreational activities, maintenance, homemaking, transportation, and protection, with the parents' siblings and grandchildren the most frequent service providers. Grandchildren helped most in areas of maintenance and transportation. There was only a small expectation of greater help from other kin if parents' needs became greater in the future. Thus, other kin are seen as occasional supplementary service providers.

Nonfamily service providers were viewed as having a relatively limited and supplementary future role as well, with each provider acting mainly in certain service areas: government help with income, home health care, transportation, protection, and housing; voluntary organizations' help for spiritual, transportation, home health care, and reading materials; friends' help for psychological support, social and recreational activities, transportation, spiritual, and reading materials services; neighbors' help for protection, homemaking, transportation, psychological support, and social and recreation activities; and hired help for home health care, maintenance, homemaking, and personal care. Very few adult children expected a great deal of help from these nonfamily providers.

In general, adult children who expect their parents to get future help from one nonfamily provider tend to expect them to get help from other providers as well. This expectation seems to be unrelated to the amount of help which they themselves feel committed to give.

The picture which emerges from the descriptive data is that adult children view themselves as being the major providers of needed services to their parents, but they do not feel committed to shoulder the whole load nor do they see siblings, other kin, or nonfamily providers as doing so.

Endnote

1. V.G. Cicirelli, "Social Services for Elderly in Relation to the Kin Network," Report to the NRTA-AARP Andrus Foundation (May, 1979).

Chapter 6

ADULT CHILDREN'S FEELINGS TOWARD THEIR ELDERLY PARENTS

The feelings which adult children have toward their elderly parents were considered in some detail in the interview questionnaire. In this chapter, various indicators of adult children's attachment to their parents will be discussed, followed by the children's feelings of filial responsibility for the parents. Next, the extent of interpersonal conflict with the parent will be considered. Finally, stress-induced personal strains and negative feelings associated with helping behaviors toward elderly parents will be presented.

Attachment Behaviors

In early childhood, two basic indicators of attachment to the parent are the proximity which the young child maintains in relation to the parent and the amount of actual contact with the parent. For the infant, proximity may be measured by the distance that the child ventures from the mother, while contact may be indicated by the amount of time during which the child is actually touching the mother. In adulthood, proximity may be measured in miles rather than in feet, but, other things being equal, the adult child who is more closely attached to the parent will be found residing at a closer physical distance. Similarly, contact in adulthood may be indicated by the frequency of visiting or telephoning the parent rather than by the time spent in actually touching the parent, but the child who is

Table 6-1   Proximity of Adult Child's Residence to that of Elderly Parent Presented in Relation to 81 Elderly Fathers and 148 Elderly Mothers

Parent's Residence	Fathers		Mothers	
	f	%	f	%
Lives with adult child	4	5	16	11
Lives in walking distance	19	23	29	20
Lives in same city (and beyond walking distance)	34	42	56	38
Lives within 50 miles (but not in same city)	6	7	12	8
Lives 50–100 miles away	2	2	4	3
Lives 100–500 miles away	8	10	14	9
Lives 500–1000 miles away	2	2	7	5
Lives over 1000 miles away	6	7	10	7

more closely attached will visit and/or telephone the parent more often.

In the present study, the adult children's proximity to parents was indicated by the distance between child's and parent's places of residence. These distances are presented in Table 6-1, summarized separately for fathers and for mothers.

The distributions of residence distances were closely similar in relation to mothers and to fathers. The most distinctive difference is that a greater percentage of elderly mothers lived with the adult children who were interviewed than did elderly fathers. This is not surprising, since a greater proportion of the elderly mothers were widowed than were the elderly fathers. Elderly parents who are both still living tend to maintain their own residence together.

Approximately 70% of the adult children lived in the same city with their parents. The largest numbers lived beyond walking distance from the parents (38% for mothers and 42% for fathers), with lesser numbers living within walking distance (20% for mothers and 23% for fathers) of the parent or actually residing with the parent (11% for mothers and 5% for fathers). Only about 20% of the adult children lived more than 100 miles away from their parents. Judged by their proximity to their parents, then, most adult children demonstrate a considerable degree of attachment to their parents.

Going on to a second type of attachment behavior, the amount of contact with the parent, the frequency of face-to-face visits with the parent was determined in the interview with the adult child. These data are summarized in Table 6-2.

The most frequent visiting pattern was to visit the elderly parents

Table 6-2   Frequency of Adult Children's Visits with 81 Elderly Fathers and 148 Elderly Mothers

Visiting with Parent	Fathers		Mothers	
	f	%	*f*	%
Lives with adult child	4	5	16	11
Every day	10	12	11	7
More than once a week	19	23	41	28
Once a week	23	28	31	21
More than once a month	8	10	11	7
About once a month	0	0	7	5
More than once a year	11	14	22	15
Once a year	5	6	7	5
Less than once a year	1	1	2	1
Not at all	0	0	0	0

once a week, or more often than once a week, but not daily. Some 51% of adult children see their fathers and 49% see their mothers that frequently. When seeing the parent daily or living with the parent are considered as well, 68% of adult children see their fathers weekly or more often and 67% see their mothers that frequently. At the other end of the continuum, only 21% of adult children see their mothers and fathers less frequently than once a month. The adult children who saw their parents less frequently tended to be the ones who also lived at greater distances from them. There were no adult children who had not seen their elderly parents within the previous two years; thus, all adult children in the study maintained some form of contact with their parents. While there are some differences in the frequencies of visiting mothers and fathers, the two distributions are remarkably similar.

A second form of contact with parents is through telephoning. Telephoning might be used as a substitute for face-to-face contact or as a supplement to it. Table 6-3 presents the frequencies of telephone calls between adult children and elderly parents.

As with visiting, the largest frequencies are for calls once a week and more often than once a week, but not daily. For these two categories of telephoning, 50% of adult children telephoned their fathers and 43% telephoned their mothers. The distributions have a secondary and smaller mode of telephoning monthly, with 16% telephoning fathers and 14% telephoning mothers that often. As with visiting, there were no adult children who did not maintain some frequency of telephoning their elderly parents.

Although it appears from inspecting Table 6-3 that adult children

Table 6-3   Frequency of Telephone Calls between Adult Children and 81 Elderly
Fathers and 148 Elderly Mothers

	Fathers		Mothers	
Telephoning Parent	*f*	*%*	*f*	*%*
Lives with adult child	4	5	16	11
Every day	5	6	21	14
More than once a week	20	25	34	23
Once a week	20	25	30	20
More than once a month	6	7	15	10
About once a month	13	16	21	14
More than once a year	10	12	9	6
Once a year	1	1	1	1
Less than once a year	2	2	1	1
Not at all	0	0	0	0

telephone their mothers more often than weekly with greater frequency than they do their fathers (48% as compared to 36%), chi-
square tests were not significant at the .05 level.

Considering all three indices of attachment behavior, it is evident
that the great majority of adult children who participated in the
study display an attachment to their elderly parents by living close
by, visiting them frequently, and telephoning them often.

Feelings of Attachment

In contrast to the attachment behaviors which involve overt acts as
indicators of the attachment bond, feelings of attachment are subjective in nature and thus more difficult to determine. The adult children's self-reports on their feelings toward their parents were
probed in the interview questionnaire and included closeness of
feeling to the parent, value consensus, compatibility of the relationship, and the perception of the parent's traits.

Closeness of feeling will be discussed first. It was measured on a
four-point scale[1] ranging from "not close at all" to "extremely close."
The frequencies and percentages of adult children expressing different degrees of closeness of feeling toward their mothers and fathers
are displayed in Table 6-4. Some 87% of adult children felt close or
extremely close to their elderly fathers, and 91% felt close or extremely close to their elderly mothers. There were 11% who felt a
little close to their fathers and 8% who felt a little close to their
mothers. Only 2% reported feeling not close at all to their elderly

Table 6-4 Adult Children's Feelings of Closeness Toward 81 Elderly Fathers and 148 Elderly Mothers

Degree of Closeness of Feeling	Fathers		Mothers	
	f	%	*f*	%
Not close at all	2	2	0	0
A little close	9	11	12	8
Close	29	36	51	34
Extremely close	41	51	85	57

Table 6-5 Adult Children's Value Consensus with 81 Elderly Fathers and 148 Elderly Mothers

Degree of Consensus	Fathers		Mothers	
	f	%	*f*	%
Don't agree at all	7	9	13	9
Agree about some things	23	28	47	32
Agree about most things	50	62	82	55
Agree completely	1	1	6	4

fathers; there were none who felt no closeness to their mothers. The mean closeness of feeling score was 3.35 (SD= 0.78) in relation to fathers and 3.49 (SD = 0.64) in relation to mothers. Most adult children feel quite close to both parents, but there is a slight tendency for adult children to feel closer to mothers.

In regard to value consensus, the degree of agreement on ideas and opinions about the things considered important in life was measured on a four-point scale[1] ranging from "don't agree at all" to "agree completely." Frequencies and percentages of adult children expressing different degrees of consensus are shown in Table 6-5. Only a very small percentage of adult children agreed completely with their parents on values, 1% agreeing with fathers and 4% with mothers. A larger number agreed about most things; 62% with fathers and 55% with mothers. A small group (9%) didn't agree at all with either mothers or fathers. The remainder agreed only about some things—28% with fathers and 32% with mothers. The mean values agreement score was 2.51 (SD = 0.81) in regard to fathers and was 2.52 (SD = 0.79) in regard to mothers. There was virtually no difference in the degree of value consensus with mothers and fathers; with both, there was only a moderate degree of values agreement.

The compatibility of the relationship between the adult child and the elderly parent was assessed by six items from the interview questionnaire. These included the adult child's perception of the satisfaction gained from the relationship, how well the adult child gets along with the elderly parent, the degree to which the parent likes to spend time with the child, the degree of the parent's interest in the child's concerns, the degree to which the child feels free to discuss topics of an intimate nature with the parent, and the extent to which the child discusses important decisions with the parent. Each was measured on a five-point scale, with "1" representing a low degree and "5" representing a high degree of the aspect of compatibility probed by the item. The scores of the six items were summed to yield a total compatibility score, with high scores indicating a relationship with high compatibility. The internal consistency reliability of the total compatibility measure, indicated by Cronbach's coefficient alpha, was .82 for the compatibility of the relationship with fathers and .74 for the compatibility of the relationship with mothers.

Means and standard deviations for the scores on the six items and the total compatibility score are presented in Table 6-6. The highest item means were found for the item asking how well the adult child gets along with parents, 4.56 (SD = 0.86) for fathers and 4.57 (SD = 0.73) for mothers. On this item, the great majority of adult children

Table 6-6   **Means and Standard Deviations for Item and Total Compatibility Scores in the Relationship with 81 Elderly Fathers and 148 Elderly Mothers**

Score	Fathers		Mothers	
	Mean	*SD*	*Mean*	*SD*
Parent takes interest in child's concerns	4.14	0.98	4.22	1.07
Child can discuss intimate topics with parent	3.27	1.55	3.43	1.53
Child gets along well with parent	4.56	0.86	4.57	0.73
Parent likes to spend time with child	4.00	0.77	4.32	0.58
Child gets satisfaction from relationship with parent	3.98	1.00	4.16	0.95
Child discusses important decisions with parent	2.28	1.19	2.08	1.26
Total compatibility	22.22	4.27	22.78	4.28

reported that they got along well or very well with their fathers (87%) and mothers (88%). In addition, item means which were approximately 4.00 and above were found for the satisfaction gained from the relationship with the parent, the degree to which the parent likes to spend time with the child, and the parent's interest in the child's concerns. Item means were lower, however, for the remaining two items. The mean for the adult child's ability to discuss intimate topics with the parent was 3.27 (SD = 1.55) in regard to the father and 3.43 (SD = 1.53) in regard to the mother. Some 19% of adult children said that they wouldn't think of bringing up such topics with their fathers, and 16% said that they wouldn't bring up intimate topics with their mothers. The mean value on this item indicates that the average adult child would bring up topics of an intimate nature with elderly parents only occasionally. The lowest item mean was found for the adult child's tendency to talk over important decisions with the parent before making them. The mean was 2.28 (SD = 1.19) for fathers and 2.08 (SD = 1.26) for mothers. These means indicate that adult children talk over important decisions with their parents only rarely. Indeed, some 36% of adult children reported never talking over decisions with their fathers and 49% reported never talking over decisions with their mothers.

The mean for the total compatibility score was 22.22 (SD = 4.27) in relation to elderly fathers and 22.78 (SD = 4.28) in relation to elderly mothers. Since total compatibility scores can range from 6 to 30, these means indicate a considerable degree of compatibility in the relationship between adult children and their elderly parents, with slightly greater feelings of compatibility with mothers than with fathers.

Perception of Parents' Traits

It was hypothesized that adult children who had positive feelings of attachment to their parents would identify more strongly with their parents and would view their traits more positively. In the questionnaire, the adult children were asked to indicate the degree to which they felt that their parents possessed each of twenty traits: fair, selfish, envious, affectionate, helpful, sarcastic, considerate, bossy, agreeable, kind, understanding, cold, suspicious, sympathetic, courteous, trustful, lazy, careless, dependable, and reasonable. The twenty traits were used in Itkin's intrafamily survey.[2] Each was rated on a five-point scale with responses ranging from "very great degree" to "slight or not at all." Scoring was reversed for negative traits, such as suspicious, so that a score of "5" in each case referred to the most positive end of the scale. A total score for the parent personality trait perceptions was obtained by summing the twenty item scores; this score could range from 20–100. Internal consistency reliability for the total score (Cronbach's coefficient alpha) was .94 in regard to the elderly father's traits and .93 in regard to the elderly mother's traits.

Means and standard deviations for the twenty item scores and for the total personality trait score in regard to the 81 elderly fathers and 148 elderly mothers of the study participants are presented in Table 6-7.

Both parents were viewed quite positively by most adult children, with all mean item scores indicating that the parents were viewed

Table 6-7   Means and Standard Deviations for 20 Personality Traits and Total Trait Score in Regard to 81 Elderly Fathers and 148 Elderly Mothers

Trait	Fathers		Mothers	
	Mean	SD	Mean	SD
Fair	4.09	0.87	3.91	0.92
Selfish*	4.15	1.06	4.23	1.01
Envious*	4.37	0.83	4.15	1.04
Affectionate	3.16	1.04	3.78	1.03
Helpful	3.93	1.07	4.08	0.88
Sarcastic*	4.06	1.20	3.92	1.27
Considerate	3.89	0.99	4.02	0.94
Bossy*	3.72	1.23	3.66	1.33
Agreeable	3.36	0.88	3.55	0.91
Kind	4.06	0.78	4.18	0.88
Understanding	3.75	0.84	3.80	1.01
Cold*	4.30	0.91	4.41	0.90
Suspicious*	3.79	1.11	3.89	1.30
Sympathetic	3.73	0.92	4.03	0.94
Courteous	4.00	0.87	4.06	0.91
Trustful	4.37	0.87	4.38	0.88
Lazy*	4.57	0.81	4.66	0.73
Careless*	4.17	0.97	4.29	0.90
Dependable	4.33	0.87	4.15	1.02
Reasonable	3.57	0.89	3.69	0.94
Total Trait Score	79.36	11.67	80.79	13.12

* Scoring for these negative traits was reversed so that "5" was the most positive end of the scale.

more positively than the "average" used as a basis of comparison. For fathers, the *least* positive trait was "affectionate," with an item mean of 3.16 (SD = 1.04), followed by "agreeable" (M = 3.36; SD = 0.88), "reasonable" (M = 3.57; SD = 0.89), "bossy" (M = 3.72; SD = 1.23), and "sympathetic" (M = 3.73; SD = 0.92). For mothers, the *least* positive trait was "agreeable" (M = 3.55; SD = 0.91), followed by "bossy" (M = 3.66; SD = 1.33), "reasonable" (M = 3.69; SD = 0.94), "affectionate" (M = 3.78; SD = 1.03), and "understanding" (M = 3.80; SD = 1.01). When scores for mothers and fathers were compared for each of the twenty traits, mothers were viewed slightly more positively than fathers for all but five traits: fair, envious, sarcastic, bossy, and dependable.

The total personality trait score in reference to elderly fathers was 79.36 (SD = 11.67); in regard to elderly mothers, it was 80.79 (SD = 13.12). Overall, as was the case with the individual item scores, both parents were perceived as having traits which were quite positive. Mothers were viewed as having slightly more positive traits than were fathers.

Filial Responsibility

The extent of the feelings of obligation which adult children feel toward their elderly parents was measured using an adaptation of the Filial Expectancy Scale.[3] (Since few children now provide financial support to parents as a consequence of the widespread acceptance of Social Security and other government programs, the item dealing with financial support to parents was deleted from the scale.) Each of the five remaining items had response alternatives ranging from "strongly agree" to "strongly disagree." The total score for filial responsibility was obtained by summing the five item scores. The scores ranged from 5 to 25, with a high score indicating a greater sense of filial responsibility toward the parent. Internal consistency reliability (Cronbach's alpha) computed for the scale was .73.

Means and standard deviations for the five items and for the total filial responsibility score are presented in Table 6-8.

Looking at the individual item means, the adult children agreed most strongly with the item concerning care for parents who are ill (M = 4.16; SD = 0.62). Next highest was the mean for feeling responsible for parents (M = 3.88; SD = 0.89), followed by visiting

Table 6-8   Means and Standard Deviations for Filial Responsibility Items and Total Score (N = 164)

Score	Mean	SD
Live close to parents	2.91	0.94
Care for parents when sick	4.16	0.62
Visit parents at least weekly	3.66	1.04
Write parents weekly	3.54	1.04
Feel responsible for parents	3.88	0.89
Total Filial Responsibility Score	18.14	3.17

weekly (M = 3.66; SD = 1.04) and writing weekly (M = 3.54; SD = 1.04). The weakest agreement was with the item about children living close to parents (M = 2.91; SD = 0.94). Overall, the total score on the scale, with a mean of 18.14 and standard deviation of 3.17, indicated only a moderate sense of responsibility toward elderly parents on the part of the adult children who were interviewed.

Interpersonal Conflict with Parents

The extent of interpersonal conflict in the relationship with elderly parents was measured by three items in the interview questionnaire: the degree of conflict in the parent-child relationship, the number of conflict areas in which the conflict typically occurs, and the degree of conflict expected if the parents lived with the adult child.

The first item, degree of conflict in the relationship, was measured on a five-point scale ranging from "none at all" to "almost every time you see each other." Frequencies and percentages of adult children reporting different extents of conflict with their elderly parents are presented in Table 6-9.

Table 6-9   Extent of Adult Children's Conflict with 81 Elderly Fathers and 148 Elderly Mothers

Extent of Conflict	Fathers		Mothers	
	f	%	f	%
None at all	29	36	57	39
Rarely	34	42	49	33
Occasionally	13	16	34	23
Frequently	4	5	8	5
Almost every time see each other	1	1	0	0

For most adult children, there is not a great deal of conflict with their elderly parents. What conflict there is occurs only rarely or occasionally, with 58% reporting rare or occasional conflict with elderly fathers and 56% reporting this level of conflict with mothers. For 36% of the participants in the study with elderly fathers, no conflict at all with fathers was found; for the 148 adult children of elderly mothers, 39% reported no conflict. At the other end of the scale, 6% of the relationships with fathers and 5% of the relationships with mothers were characterized by conflict occurring frequently or "every time we see each other." The mean score on the item was 1.94 (SD = 0.91) in regard to fathers and 1.95 (SD = 0.91) in regard to mothers. Thus, conflict did not appear to be more extensive with one parent or the other.

The second item asked for specific areas in which conflicts with the parents occurred. Responses were coded into twelve topical areas, with an additional miscellaneous category. The mean number of areas in which there was conflict between child and parent was 1.27 (SD = 1.34) in regard to fathers and 1.55 (SD = 1.78) in regard to elderly mothers. Thus, conflict with mothers tends to extend into more topical areas than did conflict with fathers. Areas of conflict are shown in Table 6-10.

Regarding conflicts with elderly fathers, the most frequently reported topic of conflict was the father's temperament (21%), followed

Table 6-10   Areas of Conflict of Adult Children with 81 Elderly Fathers and 148 Elderly Mothers

	Percentage Reporting Conflict with:	
Area of Conflict	*Fathers*	*Mothers*
Parent's criticism of child's bad habits	7	14
Parent's criticism of child's spouse	1	6
Parent's criticism of adult child's children	5	14
Parent's criticism of child's friends	2	5
Parent tells child how to live life	11	18
Parent demands too much of child	7	12
The way parent treats child's mother or father	14	7
Things child thinks parent should do	19	20
Parent's handling of money	5	6
Parent's health, taking care of self	20	23
Parent's living arrangements	2	6
Parent's temperament	21	17
Other areas (e.g., parent's ideas and opinions, relations with other family members and non-family)	10	7

by conflicts over the father's health and the way he takes care of himself (20%), conflict over things the adult child thinks the father should do (19%), the way the elderly father treats the adult child's mother (14%), and the way the father tells the adult child how to live his or her life (11%). Other conflict topics were reported in lesser degree. In the relationship with elderly mothers, the most frequent area of conflict was over the mother's health and the way she takes care of herself (23%), things the adult child thinks the elderly mother should do (20%), the way the elderly mother tells the adult child how to live his or her life (18%), the mother's temperament (17%), the mother's criticism of the adult child's bad habits (14%), the mother's criticism of the adult child's own children (14%), and the mother's excessive demands on the child (12%). Other topics of conflict were reported in lesser degree. It is apparent from Table 6-10 that while conflicts with mothers and fathers are reported to about the same extent in areas where the adult child is critical of the parent's activities, more adult children report conflicts with mothers than with fathers in areas where the elderly parent is critical or intrusive into the adult child's activities. The only area in which there was greater conflict with fathers than with mothers was over the elderly father's treatment of the mother.

The third item asked for the extent of conflict expected if the elderly parent were to live with the child. Responses are summarized in Table 6-11. No conflict at all was expected by 14% in relationships with elderly fathers and by 11% in relationships with elderly mothers, while rare or occasional conflict was expected by 64% with fathers and 51% with mothers. More frequent con-

Table 6-11   Extent of Conflict with Parent Expected by Adult Child if Parent Were to Live with Child, for 81 Elderly Fathers and 148 Elderly Mothers

	Fathers		Mothers	
Extent of Expected Conflict	*f*	*%*	*f*	*%*
Not applicable, parent already lives with child	4	5	16	11
None at all	11	14	16	11
Rarely	17	21	23	16
Occasionally	35	43	52	35
Frequently	9	11	16	11
Continual conflict, could live with it	2	2	9	6
Conflict so severe it would never work	3	4	16	11

flict was expected by 17% with fathers and 28% with mothers. Some 4% expected such severe conflict with fathers that they felt living with the parent would never work, while 11% expected conflict that severe with their mothers. The mean extent of expected conflict for those adult children whose parents did not already live with them was 2.78 (SD = 1.18; N = 77) for relationships with elderly fathers and 3.20 (SD = 1.45; N = 132) for relationships with elderly mothers. Clearly, more conflict is expected with mothers than with fathers. Also, when compared with the amount of conflict presently occurring with parents, an increase in conflict was expected if the parent should come to live with the child.

A total conflict score was obtained by summing the three item scores; for the adult children whose parents already lived with them, the future conflict was assumed to be the same as the present extent of conflict. The mean conflict score in regard to fathers was 5.96 (SD = 2.90) and the mean conflict score in regard to mothers was 6.58 (SD = 3.40). (The internal consistency reliability of the total conflict score was .80 for conflict with fathers and .71 for conflict with mothers.) For the total score as well as for the individual items, there is somewhat greater conflict with mothers than with fathers.

Personal Strains and Negative Feelings

The needs of an aging parent may place considerable stress on the adult children providing support and care in response to these needs. This may result in personal strains in the adult child and negative feelings toward the parent.

A personal strain is a cognitive awareness of tension as a result of being unable to maintain a situation or condition or to accomplish a task. Ten items in the interview questionnaire dealt with the personal strains experienced by the adult child in connection with helping or caring behavior toward elderly parents. The items used were based on adult children's complaints about helping elderly parents which were found in the literature or which were encountered in discussions with middle-aged adult children of elderly parents. The ten items are listed in Table 6-12. The interviewee was asked how much each statement applied to himself or herself, responding on a five-point scale with response alternatives ranging from "not at all" to "very much." Item scores were summed to yield a total personal strains score, with possible scores ranging from 10 to

Table 6-12   Means and Standard Deviations of Personal Strains and Negative Feelings (N = 164)

Item	Mean	SD	Some degree (% Ss)	Substantial degree (% Ss)
Physically worn out	1.56	1.03	30	11
Parent dissatisfied, no matter what one does	1.52	1.01	27	11
Strain in marriage	1.16	0.68	10	6
Can't help children as desired	1.07	0.40	9	2
Emotionally exhausted	1.60	1.12	27	16
Give up social and recreation activities	1.34	0.88	16	8
Job affected	1.13	0.58	7	2
Feel tied down	1.42	0.99	18	11
Problem in relationships with children	1.08	0.51	7	2
Financial hardship	1.08	0.41	5	1
Total Personal Strains	12.96	4.38	52[a]	34[b]
Impatient	2.20	1.39	51	33
Frustrated	2.26	1.38	52	34
Helpless	1.83	1.20	41	16
Bored	1.43	0.91	23	9
Irritated	2.17	1.37	51	31
Bitter	1.17	0.59	10	3
Hopeless	1.35	0.81	20	6
Resentful	1.27	0.75	16	5
Guilty	1.78	1.24	34	21
Angry	1.49	1.01	26	10
Total Negative Feelings	16.96	7.17	74[a]	51[b]

[a] Percentage Ss with rating of "2" or higher on one or more items.
[b] Percentage Ss with rating of "4" or higher on one or more items.

50. The internal consistency reliability (Cronbach's alpha) computed for the 164 subjects of this study was .74.

Table 6-12 presents item means and standard deviations for the ten items concerned with personal strains associated with helping behaviors toward elderly parents. In addition, the percentages of adult children reporting some degree of personal strain (a "2" or higher on the response scale) and the percentage reporting substantial strain (a "4" or "5" on the response scale) are displayed. Feeling physically worn out, emotionally exhausted, and that the elderly parent is not satisfied no matter what one does were the most frequently reported strains, followed by feeling tied down, and having to give up social and recreational activities. Financial hardship was the *least* frequently reported strain, followed by problems in the adult children's relationships with their own children, and feelings that their job is being affected. Some degree of strain was felt by from 5% of adult children (financial hardship) to 30% (feeling physically worn out), while a substantial degree of strain was felt by from 1% (financial hardship) to 16% (emotionally exhausted). Total scores on the personal strains measure were low (M = 12.96; SD = 4.38), indicating that most adult children felt only a mild level of strain, if any at all. However, 52% of the participants in the study reported some degree of strain on at least one item, and 34% reported substantial strain on at least one item.

An additional ten interview items were concerned with negative feelings experienced by adult children in connection with helping or caring behavior toward elderly parents. By the term "negative feeling" is meant an unpleasant emotional state. Like the personal strain items, the negative feeling items were based on anecdotal reports of adult children's feelings in the literature. The items, displayed in Table 6-12 in addition to the personal strain items, also used a five-point response scale ranging from "not at all" to "very much" to indicate the extent to which each item applied to the adult child. Item scores were summed to yield a total negative feelings score, with possible scores ranging from 10 to 50. The internal consistency reliability (Cronbach's alpha) for the negative feelings measure was computed as .85 for the 164 subjects of the study.

Item means and standard deviations for the ten items are also presented in Table 6-12, as well as percentages of adult children reporting some degree of negative feelings (a "2" or higher on the response scale) and the percentage reporting substantial negative feelings (a "4" or "5" on the response scale). Feeling frustrated, impatient, and irritated were the most frequently reported negative feelings, followed by feeling helpless and guilty. Feeling bitter was the least frequently reported of the ten items. Some degree of negative feelings was reported by from 10% (bitter) to 52% (frustrated), while a substantial degree of negative feelings was reported by from 3% (bitter) to 34% (frustrated). Total scores on the negative feelings measure were higher than for the personal strains measure (M = 16.96; SD = 7.17), but indicated that most adult children felt only mild levels of negative feelings. However, 73% of adult children reported some degree of negative feelings on at least one of the ten items, and 51% reported substantial negative feelings on at least one item.

Intercorrelations of Measures

Intercorrelations between the attachment behaviors (proximity to parent, frequency of visiting, and frequency of telephoning), feelings of attachment (closeness of feeling, value consensus, compatibility, and parental trait perceptions), filial responsibility, interpersonal conflict, personal strains, and negative feelings are presented in Table 6-13. The correlations among the various measures of the relationship with 81 elderly fathers are located below the diagonal of the matrix, and the correlations among the measures of the relationship with 148 elderly mothers are located above the diagonal.

The three attachment behaviors (proximity, visiting, and telephoning) are substantially interrelated, with the strongest correlations (.86 for fathers and .90 for mothers) occurring between proximity and frequency of visiting. The lowest of the correlations was between proximity and frequency of telephoning in regard to fathers (.39). Thus, those adult children who live closest to their parents are also the ones who do the most visiting and telephoning. Telephoning cannot be regarded as substitute for visiting but as a supplement to it.

The four measures of feelings of attachment (closeness of feeling, value consensus, compatibility, and parental trait perceptions) are significantly and substantially intercorrelated, both for the relationship with mothers and the relationship with fathers. The correlations ranged from .47 to .71 in the case of fathers and from .39 to .61 in the case of mothers. The strongest relationship was between closeness of feeling and compatibility of the relationship. The correlations indicate that those adult children who feel close to their elderly parents also tend to agree on values with their parents, have a more compatible relationship, and perceive their parents as having more positive traits.

The three attachment behaviors, in the relationship with fathers, are not significantly related to the feelings of attachment, with the exception of a rather weak relationship between frequency of visiting and closeness of feeling (.30) and compatibility (.23). In the relationship with mothers, these attachment behaviors are related to closeness, value consensus, and perceived personality traits, with correlations ranging from .17 to .36.

Interpersonal conflict with the parent was not significantly related to attachment behaviors, but was negatively related to feelings of attachment. For fathers, the correlations with feelings of attachment

Table 6-13 Intercorrelations Among Measures of Adult Children's Relationship with Elderly Parents

Measure	1	2	3	4	5	6	7	8	9	10	11
1. Proximity	—	.90**	.57**	.18*	.08	.05	.19*	.26**	-.12	.07	-.12
2. Visiting	.86**	—	.63**	.33**	.17*	.15	.24**	.32**	-.12	.06	-.14
3. Telephoning	.39**	.52**	—	.36**	.23**	-.12	.20*	.35**	-.01	-.11	-.11
4. Closeness of feeling	.10	.30**	.17	—	.39**	.61**	.48**	.24**	-.17*	-.08	-.19*
5. Value consensus	.11	.21	.14	.53**	—	.52**	.40**	.24**	-.23**	-.03	-.10
6. Compatibility	.07	.23*	.13	.71**	.60**	—	.60**	.36**	-.29**	-.10	-.34**
7. Parent traits	.07	.10	.02	.47**	.49**	.56**	—	.36**	-.55**	-.06	-.34**
8. Filial responsibility	.11	.21	.12	.12	.09	.17	.20	—	-.10	-.17*	-.17*
9. Conflict	.08	.01	-.08	-.30**	-.29**	-.33**	-.42**	-.02	—	.00	.33**
10. Personal strains	.12	.11	-.05	-.11	-.18	-.19	-.20	-.01	.17	—	.51**
11. Negative feelings	.10	.06	-.01	-.20	-.18	-.26*	-.24	-.04	.29**	.74**	—

* Correlation significant at the .05 level.
** Correlation significant at the .01 level.

Note: Correlations among measures of relationship with fathers located below diagonal; correlations among measures of relationship with mothers located above diagonal.

ranged from $-.29$ to $-.42$, and for mothers, the correlations ranged from $-.17$ to $-.55$. Thus, conflict tended to go hand in hand with lessened closeness, value consensus, and compatibility in the relationship, and less positive perceptions of the parent's personality traits.

Filial responsibility was not significantly related to either attachment behaviors or feelings of attachment toward the father, but was significantly related to these measures in the relationship with the elderly mother, with correlations ranging from .24 to .36. Thus, those adult children with a greater sense of filial responsibility also demonstrated more attachment behaviors and greater feelings of attachment to elderly mothers.

Personal strains and negative feelings were positively related to each other ($r = .74$ for fathers and .51 for mothers). Only negative feelings was significantly related to the extent of interpersonal conflict, however ($r = .29$ for fathers and .33 for mothers). Similarly, personal strains was not significantly related to attachment behaviors or feelings of attachment while the negative feelings measure was significantly related only to certain feelings of attachment. The correlation was $-.26$ with compatibility and $-.24$ with parental traits in the relationship with the father, and $-.19$ with closeness of feeling, $-.34$ with compatibility, and $-.34$ with parental traits in the relationship with the mother. Where there were closer feelings of attachment to the parent, there also tended to be less negative feelings associated with helping behaviors to the parent.

Summary

The adult children who were interviewed in this study showed considerable attachment behavior in their relationships with their elderly parents. The majority lived in the same city as their parents, and visited and telephoned at least weekly.

In regard to feelings of attachment, the adult children reported feeling close or extremely close to their parents and tended to agree about most values. There was considerable compatibility in the relationship with parents, with slightly greater compatibility reported with mothers. Both parents' traits were viewed quite positively by adult children, with elderly mothers seen as having slightly more positive traits than elderly fathers.

The adult children felt only a moderate sense of filial responsibility toward their parents, with the strongest feeling of responsibility directed toward caring for parents when they are sick.

Overall, there was not a great deal of conflict between adult children and their elderly parents; what conflict there was occurred only rarely or occasionally. Most adult children expected some increase in conflict if the parent were to live with them. There was slightly more conflict with mothers than with fathers.

Similarly, the amount of personal strains and negative feelings experienced by adult children in connection with helping or caring behavior toward their parents was low, indicating that such strains and negative feelings were mild for most children. However, some degree of personal strains and negative feelings was found among a substantial portion of the adult children taking part in the study.

The measures of attachment were positively intercorrelated with each other and negatively correlated with interpersonal conflict and negative feelings. Filial responsibility was not related to other measures of the relationship with elderly fathers, but was positively related in the case of elderly mothers.

Endnotes

1. B. N. Adams, *Kinship in an Urban Setting* (Chicago: Markham Publishing Co., 1968).
2. W. Itkin, "Some Relationships Between Intra-family Attitudes and Preparental Attitudes Toward Children," *Journal of Genetic Psychology*, 80 (1952), 221–252.
3. W. Seelbach and W. Sauer, "Filial Responsibility Expectations and Morale Among Aged Persons," *Gerontologist*, 17 (1977), 421–425.

Chapter 7

ADULT CHILDREN'S FEELINGS AND PROVISION OF SERVICES TO PARENTS

In earlier chapters the characteristics of adult children and their elderly parents, adult children's feelings toward elderly parents, and the extent of present and future services to parents have been described and discussed. This chapter will take up the relationships between these sets of variables. First, simple correlations between the different variable sets will be presented. Second, multiple regression analyses which consider the combined effects of selected variables will be described.

Since children's relationships with their elderly parents are a central part of these data analyses, relationships with elderly mothers and with elderly fathers are considered separately. That is, 81 adult children provided data concerning their relationships with elderly fathers and 148 provided data concerning their relationships with elderly mothers.

Data were gathered about many characteristics of adult children, their elderly parents, and the relationship between them. However, only the most important of these variables were selected for the analyses. Selection was based on the theoretical model presented in Chapter 2 and on preliminary correlational analyses.

Several groups of variables were considered in the analysis. First among these were the characteristics of the adult child: age, sex, educational level, and occupational level. Characteristics of the elderly parent used in the analyses were age, educational level, and occupational level. Sex of the parent could not be considered within the analysis itself since the analyses were carried out separately in regard to mothers and fathers.

Two measures of parental dependency were considered. The first was the adult child's global rating of the parent's dependency. The second was the total amount of the parent's service needs, as summed over the sixteen types of services.

The attachment behaviors of the adult children, including the child's proximity to the parent, the frequency of visiting, and the frequency of telephoning, were the next variables to be considered in the analysis. Based on the intercorrelations between these variables, a total score for attachment behavior was obtained by summing the three item scores. This total score was used in the regression analyses in order to avoid collinearity problems.

Feelings of attachment was represented in the analysis by four variables described earlier: closeness of feeling, values agreement, compatibility, and perception of parental traits. Again, for purposes of regression analysis, it was necessary to combine these variables to form a single score. A factor analysis revealed that there was only a single factor. Therefore, a combined factor score was constructed from the four subscores and used to represent adult children's feelings of attachment in the ensuing analyses.

Four additional measures of the parent-child relationship were also included in the analysis. These were the child's sense of filial obligation to the parent, the extent of conflict with the parent, and the personal strains and negative feelings associated with helping behavior to the parent.

The last major group of variables to be considered in the analysis was concerned with the provision of services to elderly parents. Total scores for the amount of the adult child's present helping behavior and for the extent of the adult child's commitment to provide future help to elderly parents were used in both the correlational analyses. These analyses were carried out separately for each of the sixteen types of service and for the total service score. In addition, the correlational analyses were carried out for present help and future expectation of help from siblings of the adult children and from other kin of the elderly parents. Finally, correlational analysis was made for expected future help from such nonfamily providers as government agencies, voluntary organizations, friends, neighbors, and hired help.

Since a large number of correlations was carried out, there might be cause for concern that significant findings would be merely chance occurrences. However, the number of significant correlations which were observed greatly exceeds the small number which might be expected on the basis of chance alone, and one can thus place confidence in the findings.

Correlations of Parent-Child Characteristics and Measures of Parent-Child Relationship

The intercorrelations of these variables are presented in Table 7-1. The correlations for the relationship with elderly mothers are located above the diagonal, while the correlations pertinent to the relationship with elderly fathers are found below the diagonal. (Only those correlations significant at the .05 level will be discussed.) The attachment behaviors of proximity, visiting, telephoning and the total attachment behavior score are related to both parent and child characteristics.

In the relationship with elderly mothers, sex of the adult child is weakly related to frequency of telephoning ($r = .19$), with daughters telephoning mothers more frequently than do sons. Also, older adult children both tend to live closer and to visit their mothers more frequently than do younger children ($r = .20$). Both educational ($r = -.31$) and occupational level ($r = -.16$) are related to total attachment behavior, with children at the higher educational and occupational levels displaying less attachment behavior. Age of the elderly mother ($r = .20$), occupational ($r = -.22$), and educational level ($r = -.16$) are also related to the adult child's attachment behaviors, with more proximity and visiting displayed to mothers who are older and to mothers at lower educational and occupational levels.

In the relationship with elderly fathers, only the adult child's educational level was significantly related to proximity to the parent ($r = -.30$) and frequency of visiting ($r = -.31$). Children at lower educational levels lived closer and visited their fathers more frequently than did children at higher educational levels. None of the father's characteristics were significantly related to total attachment behavior.

In the relationship with elderly mothers, both perceived dependency of the mother ($r = .30$) and the extent of the mother's needs for services ($r = .32$) were significantly related to the total attachment behavior. Thus, in the case of both parents, adult children tended to live closer and visit and telephone more frequently

Table 7-1 Intercorrelations of Child and Parent Characteristics, Parent Dependency, and Measures of the Relationship of Adult Children with Elderly Parents

Variables	Child				Parent																	
	Sex	Age	Education	Occupation	Age	Occupation	Education	Dependency	Service Need	Proximity	Visiting	Telephoning	Attachment Behaviors	Closeness	Values Agreement	Compatibility	Traits	Feelings of Attachment	Filial Obligation	Conflict	Personal Strains	Negative Feelings
Child sex	—	11	-16	-07	08	-03	03	24	22	03	15	19	14	34	17	24	08	26	05	11	21	13
Child age	07	—	-17	02	74	-23	-20	35	40	18	21	14	20	19	16	05	07	11	14	-09	29	21
Child education	-14	15	—	65	21	30	25	-20	-29	-33	-32	-17	-31	-22	-04	-02	01	-06	-04	04	-10	-03
Child occupation	-05	22	66	—	-02	14	13	-06	-04	-20	-15	-08	-16	-10	01	-01	05	-01	-05	03	-05	-04
Parent age	-15	67	15	19	—	-33	-20	42	57	20	22	11	20	17	07	-04	14	05	-01	-12	33	21
Parent occupation	-06	15	28	11	20	—	47	-15	-22	-29	-27	-01	-22	-02	02	06	-02	10	-04	12	-16	-14
Parent education	-01	09	30	10	08	50	—	-14	-23	-22	-16	-05	-16	02	12	23	14	12	-04	04	01	00
Perceived dependency	02	15	-04	01	39	06	-06	—	68	26	33	20	30	14	04	-12	05	08	13	-03	42	23
Need for service	-01	26	-16	-01	39	17	06	62	—	31	35	19	32	07	-09	-04	-11	-07	04	03	39	27
Proximity	13	-13	-30	-29	-04	-03	02	26	36	—	90	57	92	18	08	07	19	12	26	-12	07	-12
Visiting	12	-11	-31	-27	-05	06	05	32	38	86	—	63	95	33	08	23	24	24	32	-12	06	-14
Telephoning	06	-18	-05	-13	-12	10	13	13	10	39	52	—	82	36	17	13	20	33	35	-01	-11	-11
Attachment behaviors	12	-17	-26	-27	-08	05	08	28	33	88	93	75	—	32	23	17	24	25	35	-09	01	-14
Closeness	15	13	-01	00	-04	01	-01	-05	02	10	30	17	22	—	18	61	48	74	24	-17	-08	-19
Values agreement	04	24	04	-02	12	04	06	-07	03	11	21	14	18	53	—	52	40	63	24	-23	-03	-10
Compatibility	05	14	05	-01	-03	06	23	-12	-04	07	23	13	17	71	39	—	60	95	36	-29	-10	-34
Traits	04	22	08	03	-29	-05	04	11	-09	07	10	01	07	47	60	52	—	60	36	-55	-06	-34
Feelings of attachment	08	20	05	00	04	03	14	-07	-03	10	26	15	20	83	49	56	69	—	39	-37	-10	-34
Filial obligation	14	01	-02	03	-04	01	03	29	09	11	21	12	17	12	75	17	20	17	—	-10	-17	-17
Conflict	15	-18	00	13	-03	30	11	10	16	08	01	-08	00	-30	09	-33	-42	-38	-10	—	00	33
Personal strains	16	33	02	05	27	21	00	45	52	12	11	-05	07	-11	-29	-19	-20	-20	-17	17	—	51
Negative feelings	16	21	01	06	18	27	11	26	37	10	06	-01	06	-20	-18	-34	-25	-27	-04	29	74	—

Note: Correlations for 148 subjects with elderly mothers located *above* the diagonal; correlations of .16 or greater significant at the .05 level. Correlations for 81 subjects with elderly fathers located *below* the diagonal; correlations of .21 or greater significant at the .05 level.

when parents were more dependent. (As can be seen from Table 7-1, dependency is greater when elderly parents and adult children are older than is the case when they are younger. For elderly mothers, dependency is greater among those at lower educational and occupational levels.)

The overall feelings of attachment score was significantly related only to the sex of the child in the relationship with elderly mothers ($r = -.26$), with daughters feeling closer, more compatible, and having greater values agreement with their mothers than did sons. Older adult children tended to feel closer ($r = .19$) and have greater values agreement ($r = .16$) with their mothers than did younger children. Also, children at lower educational levels tended to feel closer ($r = -.22$) to their elderly mothers than did children at higher educational levels.

In the relationship with elderly fathers, none of the background variables of either parent or child were related to the overall feelings of attachment score. However, some of the specific feelings of attachment were related. Older adult children tended to have greater values agreement ($r = .24$) with their fathers and see their fathers' personality traits more positively ($r = .22$). Also, the older the father, the more positively the adult child viewed his personality traits ($r = .29$). Finally, the higher the educational level of the father, the more compatible ($r = .23$) the adult child's relationship with him.

Dependency of the parent was not significantly related to the overall feelings of attachment score (or to any of the specific feelings) in relation to either elderly mothers or elderly fathers. Thus, there is no evidence that increased dependency of the parent, in itself, is accompanied by less positive feelings of attachment to the parent.

In the relationship with elderly mothers, feelings of attachment were associated with attachment behaviors ($r = .25$), with greater feelings of attachment where there was also a greater frequency of visiting ($r = .24$) and telephoning ($r = .33$). In the relationship with elderly fathers, overall feelings of attachment were associated significantly only with visiting behavior ($r = .26$), with children who visited their fathers more frequently also reporting greater feelings of attachment.

Next to be considered is the relationship of filial obligation to attachment behaviors, feelings of attachment, and parental dependency. In the relationship of adult children with their elderly mothers, the amount of filial obligation felt by the adult child was not significantly related to the characteristics of either the adult children or their elderly mothers, or to the dependency of the mother. However, filial obligation was related to attachment behaviors ($r = .35$) and to feelings of attachment ($r = .39$), with adult children with a greater sense of filial obligation displaying more attachment behaviors and having stronger feelings of attachment.

In the case of elderly fathers, the only significant correlation with filial obligation was found with perceived dependency of the father ($r = .29$). In this relationship, adult children with a greater sense of filial obligation also perceived their fathers to be more dependent.

In regard to elderly mothers, the extent of conflict which the adult child has with the mother was not significantly related to characteristics of the adult child, characteristics of the elderly mother, dependency of the mother, the filial obligation of the adult child, or the attachment behaviors of the adult child. However, the extent of conflict was related to total feelings of attachment to the elderly mother ($r = -.37$), with adult children who reported greater amounts of conflict with their mothers also having less positive feelings of attachment.

A similar correlation between the amount of conflict and feelings of attachment ($r = -.38$) was found in the relationship of adult children with elderly fathers. Only one other correlation was significant. Adult children had more conflict with fathers of higher occupational levels than they did when fathers had lower occupational status ($r = .30$).

The personal strains and negative feelings resulting from helping behaviors toward elderly parents were correlated with characteristics of the adult child, characteristics of the elderly parent, dependency, attachment behaviors, feelings of attachment, and conflict with the parent.

In the relationship with elderly mothers, the degree of personal strain experienced by the adult child was correlated significantly with sex ($r = .21$), age of the child ($r = .29$), age of the mother ($r = .33$), occupational level of the mother ($r = -.16$), dependency of the mother ($r = .42$), amount of service needs of the mother ($r = .39$), and filial obligation ($r = -.17$). Thus, there was more personal strain experienced by daughters, by older adult children, and by children with older mothers, with mothers of lower occupational level, with mothers with greater dependency needs, with mothers with greater service needs, and by adult children who felt less filial obligation toward the parent.

In the relationship with elderly fathers, the degree of personal strain experienced by the adult child was correlated significantly with the age of the child ($r = .33$), age of the father ($r = .45$), and service needs of the father ($r = .52$). Adult children experiencing a greater degree of strain were older, had older fathers, had more dependent fathers, and had fathers with greater service needs.

Concerning mothers, the amount of negative feelings experienced by adult children was significantly correlated with the age of the adult child ($r = .21$), age of the mother ($r = .21$), dependency of the mother ($r = .23$), and service needs ($r = .27$). In addition, negative feelings were correlated with feelings of attachment ($r = -.34$), filial obligation ($r = -.17$), and conflict ($r = .33$). Adult children experiencing more negative feelings tended to be older and to have older mothers, more dependent mothers, and mothers with greater service needs. These adult children also tended to have less feelings of attachment to their mothers, less filial obligation, and more conflict.

In regard to fathers, the amount of negative feelings was correlated with occupational level of the father ($r = .27$), dependency of the father ($r = .26$), service needs ($r = .37$), feelings of attachment ($r = -.27$), and conflict ($r = .29$). Adult children experiencing more negative feelings had fathers at higher occupational levels, more dependent fathers, fathers with greater service needs, and also had less feelings of attachment to their fathers and more conflict.

Thus, personal strains and negative feelings were more extensive when elderly parents were older and more dependent. Where there were less feelings of attachment to the parents and there was more conflict in the relationship, there were also more negative feelings associated with helping behaviors.

Correlations with Present Provision of Services to Parents

The child characteristics, parent characteristics, parent dependency measures, attachment behaviors, feelings of attachment, filial expectancy, conflict, personal strains, and negative feelings which have been intercorrelated in the previous section were correlated with the helping behaviors of the child. The amount of services provided to the parent in each of 16 service areas, as well as the total amount of service, were taken as measures of the adult child's helping behaviors toward the parent. These correlations are presented in Tables 7-2 and 7-3, with Table 7-2 showing the correlations pertinent to elderly mothers and Table 7-3 showing the correlations for elderly fathers.

Overall, the amount of services which adult children provide to elderly mothers is related to sex of the adult child ($r = .19$), age of the adult child ($r = .42$), educational level of the child ($r = -.30$), age of the mother ($r = .50$), occupational level of the mother ($r = -.24$), and educational level of the mother ($r = -.17$). In general, daughters tend to provide more services to elderly mothers, and this is borne out in the specific service areas of homemaking, personal care, home health care, transportation, spiritual needs, and reading materials. Surprisingly, sons tend to provide more psychological support to their mothers than do daughters. Older adult children and those of lower educational level provide more services in almost all service areas. More services are provided to mothers who are older and of lower educational and occupational levels. Similarly, more services are provided when the adult child perceives the mother as being more dependent ($r = .58$) and having greater service needs ($r = .77$). Adult children who display more attachment behaviors ($r = .59$) also provide more services, as do those with stronger feelings of attachment ($r = .16$) and a greater sense of filial obligation ($r = .16$). The relationships with age, parent age, dependency, and attachment behaviors are also found in most of the 16 service areas (with the exception of income, employment, career education, and enrichment). The relationship with feelings of attachment was found only for the areas of maintenance, transportation, spiritual, reading materials, and enrichment services. Filial obligation was related to the provision of services only in the specific areas of maintenance, home health care, transportation, social and recreation activities, reading materials, and enrichment services. Amount of conflict was related only to the provision of spiritual services ($r = -.18$), with more services provided by adult children who had less conflict with their mothers. Finally, personal strains were associated with the provision of services ($r = .32$), particularly with homemaking, housing, personal care, home health care, transportation, psychological support, reading materials, and protection services. Negative feelings were associated only with personal care services ($r = .23$).

In regard to services to elderly fathers, the amount of service was correlated significantly with the educational level of the adult child

Table 7-2 Correlations of Measures of the Relationship and Background Characteristics with Provision of Services for 148 Adult Children with Elderly Mothers

Services	Child				Parent			Dependency	Service Need	Proximity	Visiting	Telephoning	Attachment Behaviors	Closeness	Values Agreement	Compatibility	Traits	Feelings of Attachment	Filial Obligation	Conflict	Personal Strains	Negative Feelings
	Sex	Age	Education	Occupation	Age	Occupation	Education															
Homemaking	19	39	-27	-06	47	-24	-11	56	62	48	52	34	50	18	14	08	12	13	06	-08	34	14
Housing	12	31	-21	03	32	-09	-02	34	47	41	47	39	48	15	15	08	09	12	11	-04	19	02
Income	-01	-05	-09	-05	00	05	-07	10	27	08	04	05	06	-08	-04	-06	-05	-07	04	07	-04	-05
Maintenance	-09	21	-27	-09	31	-18	-22	34	39	44	40	27	41	20	09	13	17	17	17	-04	06	01
Personal care	22	25	-13	06	39	-25	-05	45	49	25	33	14	27	06	07	-06	05	-01	-10	-08	44	23
Home health care	12	24	-13	03	35	-20	02	35	50	26	29	17	53	02	-03	-10	-06	-08	17	01	40	14
Transportation	19	34	-32	-13	45	-26	-18	45	55	46	54	42	53	26	15	12	18	19	22	-14	24	04
Psychological support	-27	16	-12	-06	21	-07	-09	48	47	27	33	23	31	18	07	12	-03	11	12	05	26	15
Social and recreation	03	29	-13	-04	22	-09	-11	27	44	24	26	27	29	09	03	11	05	11	20	-09	05	09
Employment	-11	-05	13	15	-07	-03	06	-04	06	12	09	09	-11	-08	04	10	00	05	13	01	-09	-07
Spiritual	25	30	-15	-02	28	-13	-06	27	45	33	39	22	35	10	20	13	14	16	07	-18	15	-05
Bureaucratic mediation	08	34	-16	03	37	-15	-21	34	59	26	29	20	28	24	00	16	-08	20	-01	02	14	13
Reading materials	17	38	-23	00	34	-11	-09	32	44	26	31	19	28	-09	18	07	12	02	16	-10	28	05
Career education	-01	-23	-06	02	-18	-10	09	00	-02	03	04	03	03	05	00	22	-02	02	02	-11	03	-05
Enrichment	05	-03	21	09	-07	-04	-02	08	11	18	17	20	21	12	15	02	06	18	25	-03	-09	07
Protection	10	24	-28	-11	35	-15	-09	42	55	47	50	30	47	05	05	02	05	05	10	-12	26	08
Total services	19	42	-30	-04	50	-24	-17	58	77	55	61	43	59	22	15	12	11	16	16	-10	32	12

Note: Correlations of .16 or greater significant at the .05 level.

Table 7-3 Correlations of Measures of the Relationship and Background Characteristics with Provision of Services for 81 Adult Children with Elderly Fathers

Services	Child				Parent			Dependency	Service Need	Proximity	Visiting	Telephoning	Attachment Behaviors	Closeness	Values Agreement	Compatibility	Traits	Feelings of Attachment	Filial Obligation	Conflict	Personal Strains	Negative Feelings
	Sex	Age	Education	Occupation	Age	Occupation	Education															
Homemaking	27	18	-16	-01	33	11	06	55	69	42	46	17	41	07	03	-02	-01	01	19	08	41	33
Housing	06	06	-11	00	17	14	07	46	58	32	37	41	43	-02	03	-17	-17	-12	08	07	37	29
Income	-13	-20	-07	-20	-19	-07	-09	26	42	19	22	17	23	06	08	-05	-10	-01	-02	-04	09	-06
Maintenance	-04	-04	-31	-11	27	01	-07	36	56	41	29	11	32	-16	-18	-21	-19	-22	02	26	33	24
Personal care	13	40	-08	06	27	11	-05	34	65	23	27	-11	16	19	09	06	02	11	07	08	46	25
Home health care	08	35	-02	07	29	17	11	40	75	26	31	07	25	16	11	01	-09	06	08	10	40	25
Transportation	12	20	-29	-09	32	01	-04	44	70	33	33	-07	23	00	-03	-07	-06	-06	-02	08	47	33
Psychological support	27	-07	-20	-08	-21	-16	-07	21	27	34	35	18	34	26	12	24	11	22	26	01	04	06
Social and recreation	01	13	06	-07	12	24	24	15	46	21	17	19	22	07	05	-07	-15	-04	-02	-11	34	45
Employment	-09	-21	-03	08	-15	-05	04	-01	03	09	01	09	07	-05	-07	-11	-21	-12	-10	12	00	-09
Spiritual	17	30	03	-06	33	10	13	22	36	16	17	07	16	-02	13	08	12	09	06	-18	15	11
Bureaucratic mediation	-04	15	-18	01	26	06	-02	29	67	31	35	13	31	14	05	12	-01	11	-07	06	22	17
Reading materials	-12	29	12	05	23	22	23	33	57	14	15	26	22	20	07	12	-03	12	13	-05	30	21
Career education	03	-28	-12	00	-26	03	-04	-02	05	05	02	08	06	-07	-10	-16	-31	-18	01	17	08	-04
Enrichment	16	-14	05	07	-15	07	12	-11	07	22	21	08	20	14	13	18	06	17	19	03	-06	01
Protection	-03	01	-26	-22	12	05	03	29	49	28	32	31	35	17	03	12	02	12	-03	08	17	08
Total Services	11	17	-22	-08	28	11	06	52	88	48	49	24	47	12	05	02	-09	04	10	11	46	34

Note: Correlations of .21 or greater significant at the .05 level.

($r = -.22$), age of the father ($r = .28$), perceived dependency of the father ($r = .52$), need for services ($r = .88$), and attachment behaviors ($r = .47$). More services were provided by adult children at lower educational levels, particularly maintenance, transportation, and protection. Also, more services were provided when fathers were older, more dependent, and with greater needs for services. Greater attachment behaviors were associated with greater amounts of services. Feelings of attachment were not related to the total service score, but were associated with greater amounts of psychological support ($r = .22$) and smaller amounts of maintenance services ($r = -.22$). Greater filial obligation was related to greater psychological support ($r = .26$), and conflict with the father was associated with greater provision of maintenance services ($r = .26$). Both personal strains ($r = .46$) and negative feelings ($r = .34$) were associated with the provision of services. In particular, personal strains were associated with homemaking, housing, income, maintenance, personal care, home health care, transportation, social and recreation activities, and reading materials services. Negative feelings were associated with homemaking, housing, maintenance, personal care, home health care, transportation, and social and recreation services.

In regard to both elderly mothers and elderly fathers, provision of services was greater at lower socioeconomic levels, when parents were older, more dependent, and in greater need of services, and when there were more attachment behaviors. Feelings of attachment and filial obligation were related to provision of services to mothers more than they were in the case of fathers, although there were some weak relationships in regard to fathers. Finally, personal strains and negative feelings were more strongly associated with services to elderly fathers than they were with services to elderly mothers.

Correlations with Commitment to Provide Future Services

The same variables which were correlated with the present provision of services to parents by adult children were also correlated with the commitment to provide future services. This commitment was assessed in regard to a hypothetical future situation when the parents' needs for service would be great. These correlations are presented in Tables 7-4 and 7-5. Table 7-4 presents the correlations in regard to mothers while Table 7-5 presents the correlations in regard to fathers.

The correlations in relation to elderly mothers will be discussed first. Characteristics of the adult child and characteristics of the parent were not significantly related to the total score for commitment to provide future services. There were, however, a few scattered correlations with particular services, such as daughters' greater commitment to provide housing ($r = .24$), psychological support ($r = .32$), and personal care ($r = .20$). The total score for commitment to provide future services was related to both perceived dependency of the parent ($r = .23$) and present service needs of the parent ($r = .16$). Commitment to provide future services was more strongly related to present attachment behaviors ($r = .58$), feelings of attachment ($r = .36$), filial obligation ($r = .29$), and present conflict with the mother ($r = -.27$). Greater attachment behaviors, closer feelings of attachment, and greater filial obligation were all associated with greater commitment to provide future services. This was found in most of the 16 service areas as well as with the total score. However, the relationship of conflict to lessened commitment to provide future services was borne out only in the specific service areas of personal care, home health care, maintenance, transportation, social and recreation, spiritual, and bureaucratic mediation services. Finally, while personal strains and negative feelings associated with present services to elderly mothers were not related to overall future commitment, greater negative feelings were associated with weaker commitment to provide future home health care and transportation services.

The commitment to provide future services to elderly fathers was significantly related to age of the adult child ($r = -.34$), age of the elderly father ($r = -.26$) and attachment behaviors ($r = .51$). Older children and those with older fathers had less commitment to provide future services, while those who displayed greater attachment behaviors had a greater commitment to provide future services to elderly fathers. There were significant correlations in specific service areas as well. Daughters were more committed to provide personal care, home health care, and psychological support to their fathers than were sons. Adult children at lower educational and occupational levels had a greater commitment to provide personal care, transportation, social and recreation activities and protection to the elderly fathers. Those with greater feelings of attachment had a

Table 7-4 Correlations of Measures of the Relationship and Background Characteristics with Commitment to Provide Future Services for 148 Adult Children with Elderly Mothers

Services	Child				Parent					Proximity	Visiting	Telephoning	Attachment Behavior	Closeness	Values Agreement	Compatibility	Traits	Feelings of Attachment	Filial Obligation	Conflict	Personal Strains	Negative Feelings
	Sex	Age	Education	Occupation	Age	Occupation	Education	Dependency	Service Need													
Homemaking	07	00	-19	-09	04	-15	00	21	15	53	51	45	56	21	10	27	30	29	20	-13	-04	-15
Housing	24	02	04	14	05	04	17	24	16	22	28	28	29	20	18	29	31	31	23	-12	04	05
Income	05	09	15	17	13	-05	04	20	28	08	06	15	11	03	10	17	15	16	07	-15	20	03
Maintenance	-14	07	-04	01	08	-15	-02	15	08	47	39	29	43	12	08	12	26	16	24	-18	-04	-07
Personal care	20	06	-19	-11	-09	-20	00	23	15	36	41	28	39	21	19	18	33	26	23	-24	11	-10
Home health care	17	13	-10	-06	13	-07	08	15	13	38	42	42	45	28	29	30	31	36	27	-17	07	-19
Transportation	02	02	-15	-04	01	-11	-01	17	08	53	52	43	55	21	28	28	32	33	30	-27	03	-27
Psychological support	32	07	-13	-08	16	-05	-05	26	26	30	35	37	38	26	11	32	25	32	15	-10	12	-04
Social and recreation	13	09	-09	-03	06	-06	06	17	17	37	37	43	43	16	12	20	25	23	20	-20	01	01
Employment	-03	-11	10	20	-15	-02	09	-03	-07	17	20	26	23	07	14	14	05	09	05	-08	-10	-03
Spiritual	14	11	-03	06	11	-08	-01	20	11	37	40	27	39	17	23	28	37	32	17	-21	-01	12
Bureaucratic mediation	-03	15	-04	-04	10	-11	-10	13	17	35	32	29	36	10	10	07	14	11	25	-06	-03	-07
Reading materials	14	07	05	10	-03	07	08	03	-04	26	30	23	33	26	24	24	19	28	25	-06	-01	-03
Career education	13	-07	03	10	-08	-06	02	05	-04	15	16	23	20	09	17	06	06	09	01	-09	01	07
Enrichment	06	-12	06	06	-03	01	04	11	05	12	10	15	14	06	10	17	12	16	08	-06	-05	03
Protection	05	10	-25	-09	10	-19	-08	20	12	56	56	38	56	19	19	15	23	21	29	29	-05	-20
Total future services	14	08	-08	03	07	-12	03	23	16	52	54	49	58	26	26	31	36	36	29	27	02	-13

Note: Correlations of .16 or greater significant at the .05 level.

Table 7-5   Correlations of Measures of the Relationship and Background Characteristics with Commitment to Provide Future Services for 81 Adult Children with Elderly Fathers

Services	Child				Parent					Proximity	Visiting	Telephoning	Attachment Behavior	Closeness	Values Agreement	Compatibility	Traits	Feelings of Attachment	Filial Obligation	Conflict	Personal Strain	Negative Feelings
	Sex	Age	Education	Occupation	Age	Occupation	Education	Dependency	Service Need													
Homemaking	17	-38	-21	-18	-25	-06	08	12	21	49	43	27	47	02	04	07	-06	04	09	13	02	15
Housing	10	-14	06	03	-12	-11	-01	23	15	21	21	11	21	10	16	06	11	11	11	00	-02	00
Income	01	-17	15	12	-12	08	05	09	-06	-01	-06	07	01	-13	-07	03	06	-02	13	12	12	07
Maintenance	-13	-22	-06	-10	-04	08	03	19	19	46	41	23	43	-03	01	02	-09	-01	12	14	-04	01
Personal care	25	-18	-26	-25	-20	-16	-13	12	17	39	42	17	38	25	24	15	10	21	17	03	-04	-06
Home health care	23	-19	-10	-13	-08	01	01	08	16	36	40	29	41	16	31	08	01	15	32	04	03	06
Transportation	09	-26	-22	-15	-19	-07	05	14	16	49	49	25	48	20	25	21	07	23	22	-01	-04	-08
Psychological support	27	-24	-20	-18	-23	11	01	07	18	44	42	26	44	11	09	07	-11	07	08	04	01	06
Social and recreation	10	-22	-05	-27	-22	26	21	-04	04	35	27	28	35	-07	03	-09	-14	-08	06	10	-12	-01
Employment	-08	-25	13	16	-24	-01	-09	-17	-20	06	08	13	10	07	04	-12	-20	-07	-02	00	-19	-16
Spiritual	14	-14	-01	-16	-03	00	11	00	06	31	33	28	36	23	30	18	05	23	07	-03	-17	-09
Bureaucratic mediation	-09	-11	-17	-14	00	-15	-17	14	11	30	30	11	28	04	09	-02	10	03	16	-13	-19	-28
Reading materials	08	-13	00	-16	-24	07	08	01	-03	29	26	19	29	12	18	19	03	18	26	-07	-07	02
Career education	09	-23	08	09	-22	08	-02	-14	-07	10	04	02	06	-15	-10	-20	-32	-22	05	14	-07	00
Enrichment	-03	32	-07	-14	-28	14	27	03	15	20	17	10	18	02	-06	10	-06	04	11	03	-01	12
Protection	03	-16	-30	-40	-18	-08	03	01	05	46	44	21	43	11	10	13	05	13	13	00	-12	-11
Total future services	13	-34	-12	-18	-26	00	04	10	13	51	48	31	51	12	18	08	-04	10	22	06	-10	-04

Note: Correlations of .21 or greater significant at the .05 level.

greater commitment to provide future transportation and spiritual services to their elderly fathers. Those with greater filial obligation showed a greater commitment to provide future home health care, transportation, and reading materials for their fathers. Those with greater negative feelings associated with providing services at present had less commitment to provide bureaucratic mediation services in the future.

Commitment to provide future services was most strongly related to present attachment behaviors in regard to both mothers and fathers. Commitment to help elderly mothers was also related to present dependency and need for services, feelings of attachment, filial obligation, and conflict, while commitment to help elderly fathers was related to these variables only through scattered correlations in particular service areas. By contrast, age of child and age of parent were related to the commitment to provide future services to fathers but not to mothers.

Correlations with Services from Other Providers

Adult children of the elderly were asked about the amount of services which their parents received at the present time from the adult children's brothers and sisters and from other kin. They were also asked about the amount of help which they felt that their parents might expect in the future (in a hypothetical situation where a great deal of help was needed) from siblings, other kin, government agencies, voluntary organizations, friends, neighbors, and hired service providers. Total scores for present and expected future services from these other providers were correlated with characteristics of the adult child, characteristics of the parent, and various measures of the adult child's relationship with the elderly parent. These correlations are presented in Tables 7-6 and 7-7, with Table 7-6 dealing with present services and Table 7-7 dealing with expected future services.

Present help from the adult child's siblings is first to be considered. Characteristics of the adult child were not significantly related to the amount of help which the adult child's siblings provided to the elderly mother. However, the mother's age ($r = .25$), educational level ($r = -.16$), dependency ($r = .47$), and need for services ($r = .37$) were significantly related to services. Siblings provided more help to elderly mothers who were older, at a lower educational

Table 7-6 Correlations of Measures of the Relationship and Background Characteristics with Total Scores for Present Services and Expected Future Services from Other Providers for 148 Adult Children with Elderly Mothers

Provider	Child				Parent					Proximity	Visiting	Telephoning	Attachment Behavior	Closeness	Values Agreement	Compatibility	Traits	Feelings of Attachment	Filial Obligation	Conflict	Personal Strains	Negative Feelings
	Sex	Age	Education	Occupation	Age	Occupation	Education	Dependency	Service Need													
Present																						
Siblings[a]	14	18	-09	02	25	-11	-16	47	37	03	05	-05	08	11	09	12	-06	14	04	-07	20	23
Other kin	20	09	02	03	21	-08	-10	29	24	15	19	16	19	13	09	11	11	13	12	07	14	03
Future																						
Brothers[b]	06	-09	13	06	-14	10	09	-05	-11	-10	-06	-09	-06	04	04	14	09	37	13	-18	-14	-12
Sisters[c]	-05	-14	-04	02	03	-13	-05	02	-04	01	-01	07	-09	24	16	18	12	22	-09	-21	-01	-02
Other kin	16	04	12	12	07	00	-11	-03	-03	10	12	15	14	15	15	14	14	17	05	-01	00	-04
Government agencies	04	-25	05	-14	-25	13	-04	06	-08	-02	-02	01	-01	-14	-05	02	-06	-03	07	18	-05	02
Voluntary organizations	-02	-24	15	01	-26	18	02	04	-10	-01	01	01	00	-18	-03	-02	-09	-07	02	12	-10	00
Friends	-12	-27	27	21	-36	21	14	-22	-33	-17	-15	-01	-13	-06	15	19	07	14	10	03	-29	-08
Neighbors	-08	-13	14	06	-29	13	01	-14	-27	-14	-11	-05	-11	-05	06	12	-05	07	08	07	-18	-05
Hired help	-03	-06	26	14	-07	12	15	00	02	-25	-29	-26	-29	-27	-14	-22	-19	-25	-07	12	09	28

Note: Correlations of .16 or greater significant at the .05 level.
a N = 125
b N = 87
c N = 94

Table 7-7 Correlations of Measures of the Relationship and Background Characteristics with Total Scores for Present Services and Expected Future Services from Other Providers for 81 Adult Children with Elderly Fathers

Provider	Child				Parent																		
	Sex	Age	Education	Occupation	Sex	Occupation	Education	Dependency	Service Need	Proximity	Visiting	Telephoning	Attachment Behavior	Closeness	Values Agreement	Compatibility	Traits	Feelings of Attachment	Filial Obligation	Conflict	Personal Strains	Negative Feelings
Present																						
Siblings[a]	00	24	-06	09	35	05	-05	40	52	09	06	-17	03	-07	-01	00	04	05	23	20	24	15
Other kin	11	05	00	00	17	01	03	33	27	19	15	04	15	00	-11	05	13	03	18	02	19	13
Future																						
Brothers[b]	-05	-13	-16	-28	-01	-06	-02	-10	-04	-06	00	-01	-06	20	14	13	21	21	19	-13	-14	-21
Sisters[c]	-19	-14	03	06	-04	-08	-10	-05	-16	-16	-26	-28	-25	-20	-19	-17	-09	-21	-16	20	-08	-12
Other kin	14	-10	18	07	-07	04	21	-03	-06	04	07	13	09	06	03	21	11	15	17	-02	-06	07
Government agencies	08	-10	05	-10	-22	14	08	10	21	09	06	-14	00	01	-07	-06	-02	-05	-03	-02	16	10
Voluntary organizations	05	-21	06	-17	-32	17	08	01	04	04	-04	-04	-01	-06	-07	-06	-05	-07	07	-06	08	16
Friends	03	-29	18	16	-34	14	19	-26	-25	-29	-35	-19	-33	-15	-21	-09	-17	-16	07	14	-20	-01
Neighbors	03	-14	11	07	-30	10	25	-22	-24	-31	-28	-13	-29	06	-05	16	04	10	09	-12	-21	-07
Hired help	-02	-13	24	07	-09	40	25	-10	-17	-14	-16	-05	-14	-06	00	01	05	00	05	12	-08	-07

Note: Correlations of .21 or greater significant at the .05 level.
[a] N = 71
[b] N = 55
[c] N = 49

level, who were more dependent, and who had greater needs for service. Adult children who experienced greater personal strains and negative feelings when helping their mothers also tended to have siblings who provided more help to the elderly mothers ($r = .20$ with personal strains, and $r = .23$ with negative feelings).

The amount of help received by elderly fathers from the adult child's siblings was related to age of the adult child ($r = .24$), age of the father ($r = .35$), dependency of the father ($r = .40$), service needs of the father ($r = .52$), filial obligation of the adult child ($r = .23$), and personal strains experienced by the adult child ($r = .24$). More help was given by siblings when the adult child was older, had a greater sense of filial obligation, and experienced more personal strains in providing help to the fathers. Also, more help was given by siblings when the elderly father was older, more dependent, and with greater needs for services.

Adult children were asked to indicate separately the amount of help which they could expect their brothers and sisters to give to their elderly parents. In regard to mothers, adult children with greater feelings of attachment to their mothers expected their brothers ($r = .37$) and their sisters ($r = .22$) to provide more future services to their mothers. In addition, adult children who had less conflict with their mothers ($r = -.21$) expected their sisters to provide more services to their mothers. In regard to fathers, children at lower occupational levels expected their brothers ($r = -.28$) to provide more future services to their elderly fathers. Also, adult children who displayed less attachment behaviors (particularly visiting and telephoning) expected their sisters to provide more future services to their fathers.

The study was also concerned with services which elderly parents received from kin other than their children. This included the elderly parents' sisters, brothers, cousins, aunts, uncles, nieces, nephews, grandchildren, more distant kin, and kin through marriage. In regard to elderly mothers, sex of the adult child ($r = .20$), attachment behaviors ($r = .19$), age of the mother ($r = .21$), dependency of the mother ($r = .29$) and service needs ($r = .24$) were significantly related to the services which the elderly mother presently received from kin other than her children. Older, more dependent mothers with greater needs for services received more help from these other kin. Further, daughters and adult children displaying more attachment behaviors reported that their mothers received more kin services than did sons or children manifesting less attachment behaviors. Services from other kin to elderly fathers were significantly related only to the elderly fathers' dependency ($r = .33$) and needs for services ($r = .27$), with more help from other kin going to elderly fathers who are more dependent and have greater service needs.

When future services from other kin were considered, sex of the adult child ($r = .16$) and feelings of attachment ($r = .17$) were weakly related to the amount of future services to mothers expected from other kin, with daughters and adult children with greater feelings of attachment expecting more help from other kin. None of the variables were significantly correlated with the amount of future help to fathers expected from other kin.

Next, future help from the various nonfamily providers will be discussed, beginning with services from government agencies. In regard to elderly mothers, age of the adult child ($r = -.25$), age of the mother ($r = -.25$), and amount of conflict with the mother ($r = .18$) are the only variables significantly correlated with the amount of future services expected from government agencies. Greater amounts of future services from government were expected by younger adult children, children with younger mothers, and children who have more conflict with their mothers. In regard to elderly fathers, age of the father ($r = -.22$) was the only variable related to expected future services from government agencies, with more future services expected by adult children with younger fathers.

For future services from voluntary organizations, age of the adult child ($r = -.24$), age of the elderly mother ($r = -.26$), and occupational level of the mother ($r = .18$) were significantly correlated with expected future services from voluntary organizations. Younger adult children, those with younger mothers, and those with mothers at higher occupational levels expected more future services from voluntary organizations. In regard to elderly fathers, age of the father was the only variable significantly related to expected services ($r = .32$), with adult children with younger fathers expecting them to get more future services from voluntary organizations.

The amount of future help expected for elderly mothers from their friends was significantly related to age of the adult child ($r = -.27$), educational level of the child ($r = .27$), occupational level of the child ($r = .21$), age of the mother ($r = -.36$), occupational level of the mother ($r = .21$), dependency of the mother ($r = -.22$), service needs of the mother ($r = -.33$), and personal strain experienced by the adult child ($r = -.29$). Thus, adult children who expected their elderly mothers to receive more help from friends were younger, at higher educational and occupational levels, and experienced less personal strains in helping their mothers. Their mothers tended to be younger, at higher occupational levels, and less dependent with fewer needs for services. In regard to elderly fathers, age of the adult child ($r = -.29$), age of the father ($r = .34$), dependency of the father ($r = -.26$), service needs ($r = -.25$), and attachment behaviors ($r = -.33$) were related to the amount of future help expected from friends. Adult children who were younger, who had fewer attachment behaviors, and whose fathers were younger, less dependent, and with less need for services expected more future help for their fathers from friends.

Expected future help from neighbors was correlated with the age of the mother ($r = -.29$), service needs of the mother ($r = -.27$), and personal strains ($r = -.18$). More help was expected for elderly mothers from neighbors in the future when the mother is younger, with fewer needs for services, and when the adult children experience less personal strains in helping their mothers. Regarding elderly fathers, expected help from neighbors was significantly related to age of the elderly father ($r = -.30$), educational level of the father ($r = .25$), dependency ($r = -.22$), service needs ($r = -.24$), and attachment behaviors of the adult child ($r = -.29$). More future help was expected from neighbors when the elderly father was younger, of higher educational level, less dependent, with less service needs, and when the adult child displayed less attachment behaviors.

The last of the nonfamily service providers to be considered in the study was the hired provider. The amount of future help to elderly mothers expected from hired providers was related to educational level of the child ($r = .25$), attachment behaviors of the child ($r = -.29$), feelings of attachment ($r = -.25$), and negative feelings ($r = .28$). Adult children at higher educational levels, lower amounts of attachment behaviors, less feelings of attachment, and more negative feelings associated with helping behavior expect more future services to their mothers from hired providers. In regard to elderly fathers, the amount of future help expected from hired providers was related only to educational level of the adult child ($r = .24$), and occupational ($r = .40$) and educational levels ($r = .25$) of the fathers. Thus, those at higher socioeconomic status levels expect greater amounts of future services from hired providers for their elderly fathers.

Multiple Regression Analyses

Thus far, only the zero-order correlations between variables have been considered, in which the relationships between variables are taken for each pair of variables. For determining the combined effect of several variables, multiple regression analysis was used. Selection of variables for regression analyses was based on two main considerations. The first was the theoretical interest in the variables (as presented in Chapter 2). The second was a more practical consideration, based on measurement characteristics of the variables and their intercorrelations. Where two or more variables were strongly correlated, either a single score was constructed (e.g., the factor score for attachment feelings) or a single variable was selected to represent both.

Four variables were selected as measures of the relationship of adult children with their elderly parents: attachment behaviors, feelings of attachment, filial obligation, and conflict. (Personal strains and negative feelings were not included as predictors of services to parents because they were considered to be consequents of such services.) In addition, the perceived dependency of the parent was included in the analyses. These five variables, then, were the main predictors of child services to parents which were investigated in the multiple regression analyses.

The set of child characteristics (sex, age, educational and occupational levels) were also considered in the multiple regression analyses. These background variables were entered into the regression first, followed by the five main variables.

Two regression analyses are presented. The first considers the effect of the five main variables; the second considers the effect of the five main variables after the effect of the child background characteristics has been taken into account. (A third analysis similarly considered the effect of the parent background characteristics; however, little additional information was gained and this analysis will not be presented here.)

The first of the regression analyses was concerned with the prediction of present provision of services from measures of the relationship with the elderly mother. A summary of the regression is presented in Table 7-8. The proportion of variance accounted for by significant predictors is included in the table along with the multiple regression coefficient (R). The regressions for the total amount of

Table 7-8 Summary of Regressions of Amount of Service Provided on Measures of the Relationship and Child Characteristics for 148 Adult Children with Elderly Mothers

Service	Dependency	Conflict	Filial Obligation	Attachment Behaviors	R	Sex	Age	Education	Dependency	Conflict	Filial Obligation	Attachment Behaviors	Feelings of Attachment	R
Homemaking	.32			.14	.68		.14	.04	.17			.11		.70
Housing	.11			.15	.52		.09	.05	.04			.12		.57
Maintenance	.12		.03	.09	.48	.01	.05	.07	.08			.07	.02	.57
Personal care	.21		.05	.04	.53	.05	.05		.13		.02	.03		.57
Home health care	.12			.07	.49		.05		.08		.04	.06		.51
Transportation	.20			.14	.62		.10	.05	.08			.10		.65
Psychological support	.23			.03	.52	.08			.16			.03		.54
Social and recreation	.07			.03	.36		.08		.03			.02		.41
Spiritual	.07	.03		.08	.43	.06	.08			.03		.06		.50
Bureaucratic mediation	.11			.05	.41		.11	.02	.05			.04		.49
Reading materials	.10			.02	.40		.13	.04	.02					.50
Protection	.18			.13	.57		.05	.04	.10			.10		.58
Total services	.33			.18	.73		.16	.06	.16			.14		.76

Note: Proportion of variance accounted for is given for significant predictors.

child services to elderly mothers is summarized in the table, as well as regressions for 12 of the 16 specific service areas (regressions for income, employment, career education, and enrichment services were not significant and are not included in the table). The analyses for the specific service areas are included only to provide diagnostic information; the analysis for the total service score is the primary analysis. Overall, perceived dependency of the mother and attachment behaviors of the adult child are the two major predictors of the adult child's provision of services to the elderly mother, both before and after child characteristics are taken into account. Age and educational level of the adult child are significant background characteristics. Sex of the child enters into regressions for maintenance, personal care, psychological support, and spiritual services, but not into the total child services. Similarly, filial obligation makes a significant contribution to personal care and home health care, while feelings of attachment are related to maintenance services. Overall, the multiple R was .76, indicating that 58% of the variance in the total child services score was accounted for by the predictors.

A summary of the regression analyses for the present provision of services to elderly fathers is presented in Table 7-9. Regressions for the total service score and the 12 specific services listed above are included. As with the analyses for mothers, dependency of the father and the child attachment behaviors are the two major predictors of child services, with educational level of the child the only background variable which was significant in the overall analysis. Parent dependency and child attachment behaviors were also significant predictors in most of the 12 specific service areas. However, educational level was a significant predictor only for transportation and bureaucratic mediation services. Sex of the adult child was a predictor of homemaking, maintenance, and psychological support, while age of the adult child was important in personal care, home health care, transportation, and reading materials services. The multiple R for the overall child services score was .68, indicating that 46% of the variance was accounted for by the predictors.

A summary of the regression analyses for the adult child's commitment to provide future services to elderly mothers is presented in Table 7-10. Regressions for the total future service score and for the 12 specific service areas for which the analyses were significant are included in the table. The adult child's attachment behaviors are the strongest predictor of commitment to provide future help to elderly mothers, with conflict with the mother a second major pre-

Table 7-9 Summary of Regressions of Amount of Service Provided on Measures of the Relationship and Child Characteristics of 81 Adult Children with Elderly Fathers

Service	Dependency	Filial Obligation	Attachment Behaviors	R	Sex	Age	Education	Dependency	Feelings of Attachment	R
Homemaking	.30		.07	.61	.07			.23	.07	.68
Housing	.21		.12	.59				.19	.13	.61
Maintenance	.13		.08	.52	.11			.11	.05	.59
Personal care	.11			.38		.15		.08		.55
Home health care	.16			.44		.12		.12	.05	.57
Transportation	.19			.48		.05	.08	.17		.59
Psychological support			.06	.44	.07				.06	.50
Social and recreation		.04	.04	.28					.05	.39
Bureaucratic mediation	.08		.05	.44		.09	.07	.09	.05	.52
Reading materials	.11			.38				.08	.04	.50
Protection	.08		.07	.45				.10	.04	.51
Total services	.27		.11	.63			.04	.24	.11	.68

Note: Proportion of variance accounted for is given for significant predictors.

Table 7-10   Summary of Regressions of Commitment to Provide Future Services on Measures of the Relationship and Child Characteristics for 148 Adult Children with Elderly Mothers

Service	Dependency	Conflict	Attachment Behaviors	Feelings of Attachment	R	Sex	Education	Dependency	Conflict	Attachment Behaviors	Feelings of Attachment	R
Homemaking	.06		.23	.02	.58	.06	.03			.21	.02	.60
Housing		.03	.03	.04	.42			.04		.04	.02	.49
Maintenance		.06	.11		.46					.13		.51
Personal care			.08		.47	.04			.06	.06		.50
Home health care			.13	.04	.52	.03				.12		.53
Transportation		.07	.20		.61		.02			.19		.63
Psychological support	.06		.08	.06	.48	.10			.06	.07	.03	.52
Social and recreation			.12		.47					.12		.48
Spiritual		.10	.08		.51				.09	.08		.53
Bureaucratic mediation		.04	.08		.41				.03	.09		.43
Reading materials			.07	.03	.40		.05			.08		.44
Protection		.08	.20		.62				.06	.17		.62
Total future services		.07	.21	.02	.64				.06	.21		.65

Note: Proportion of variance accounted for is given for significant predictors.

dictor. None of the child background characteristics was significant in the overall regression, although sex of the child was important in housing, personal care, home health care, and psychological support services, and educational level was important in homemaking, transportation, and protection services. The adult child's attachment behaviors were important predictors in all 12 types of services, while conflict was a significant predictor only for personal care, transportation, spiritual, bureaucratic mediation, and protection services. In addition, the mother's dependency was significant in the regression for housing, and feelings of attachment was a significant predictor of homemaking, housing, home health care, and psychological support. The multiple R was .65, indicating that 42% of the variance in the total score for the child's commitment to provide future services to the mother was explained by the predictors.

Table 7-11 presents a summary of the regression analyses for the adult child's commitment to provide future services to elderly fathers. Included are the regressions for the total future service scores and for 11 of the 16 specific service areas for which the regressions are significant (housing, income, employment, career education, and enrichment services are not included). As with elderly mothers, the adult child's present attachment behaviors are the strongest predictor of commitment to provide help in the future. Age of the adult child is a significant background variable in the overall regression, but it enters into regression only in the areas of homemaking, transportation, and psychological support. Sex of the adult child is significant in the areas of personal care, home health care, and psychological support, while educational and occupational levels enter into social and recreational services. Filial obligation is a significant predictor of home health care and reading materials services, and feelings of attachment are predictors of personal care and transportation services. The multiple R was .60, indicating that the predictors accounted for 36% of the variance in the total score for adult children's commitment to provide future services to elderly fathers.

Regression analyses were also carried out to determine the extent to which personal strains and negative feelings could be predicted from the amount of services which adult children provided for their elderly parents and from the measures of the relationship to parents (attachment behaviors, feelings of attachment, filial obligation, conflict), perceived dependency of the parent, and child background characteristics. Table 7-12 presents summaries of these regressions in regard to elderly mothers and elderly fathers.

Table 7-11 Summary of Regressions of Commitment to Provide Future Services on Measures of the Relationship and Child Characteristics for 81 Adult Children with Elderly Fathers

Service	Filial Obligation	Attachment Behaviors	R	Sex	Age	Education	Occupation	Filial Obligation	Attachment Behaviors	Feelings of Attachment	R
Homemaking		.20	.49		.14				.09		.59
Maintenance		.16	.46						.12	.05	.52
Personal care		.10	.43	.06					.03		.52
Home health care	.08	.13	.50	.05				.08	.08		.53
Transportation		.17	.52		.06				.09		.58
Psychological support		.18	.44		.05				.10	.07	.53
Social and recreation		.16	.43	.07					.10		.52
Spiritual		.11	.40			.03	.07		.07		.45
Bureaucratic mediation		.06	.34						.04		.38
Reading materials	.05	.06	.39						.04		.44
Protection		.18	.46				.16	.07	.09		.55
Total future services	.03	.23	.54		.10				.14		.60

Note: Proportion of variance accounted for is given for significant predictors.

Helping Elderly Parents

Table 7-12   Summary of Regressions of Personal Strains and Negative Feelings on Amount of Services Provided by Adult Children, Measures of the Relationship, and Child Characteristics for 148 Adult Children with Elderly Mothers and 81 Adult Children with Elderly Fathers

Variable	Personal Strains		Negative Feelings	
	Fathers	*Mothers*	*Fathers*	*Mothers*
Child services	.17	.02	.09	
Feelings of attachment	.08		.10	.05
Filial obligation		.05		
Conflict				.10
Attachment behaviors				.03
Dependency	.04	.10		.03
Sex		.04		
Age	.10	.07		.04
Education				
Occupation				
Multiple R	.65	.55	.54	.56

Note: Proportion of variance accounted for is given for significant predictors.

The amount of services provided by the child, the perceived dependency of the parent, and the age of the adult child were significant predictors of the amount of personal strain associated with helping behaviors to the parent. This was the case both in the analysis of the data regarding elderly mothers and the data regarding elderly fathers. Concerning mothers, filial obligation and sex of the adult child also predicted the amount of personal strain reported. In the cases of the regression analysis concerning elderly fathers, feelings of attachment was also a significant predictor of personal strains. The multiple R was .65 for fathers and .55 for mothers.

Going on to the regression analyses for negative feelings, the analysis in regard to elderly fathers will be considered first. The amount of services provided and the adult child's feelings of attachment were the only significant predictors of negative feelings associated with helping behaviors. The situation was more complex in regard to elderly mothers. Amount of service provided was not a significant predictor, while amount of conflict with the mother was a major predictor, followed in importance by feelings of attachment, attachment behaviors, perceived dependency of the mother, and age of the adult child. The multiple R was .54 for the regression regarding elderly fathers and .56 in regard to elderly mothers.

Causal Model

In Chapter 2, a model of variables influencing helping behavior toward elderly parents and based on attachment theory was proposed. A major feature of this model was the notion that feelings of attachment were causally antecedent to attachment behaviors, and, in turn, to helping behaviors. In turn, both were regarded as causally antecedent to the commitment to provide help in time of future need.

The method of path analysis was used to explore the nature of these hypothesized causal connections between the main variables of interest to the study. Figure 7-1 presents the path diagram resulting from the analysis. All paths with path coefficients less than .10 have been deleted from the diagram as being of negligible importance. (Also, personal strains and negative feelings have been omitted from Figure 7-1 in the interest of visual clarity. This was possible since personal strains and negative feelings had a negligible causal effect on future commitment to help, and thus could be viewed as simple consequents of present helping behaviors and other prior variables in the causal chain.) Finally, Figure 7-1 presents the analysis in relation to elderly mothers. The path diagram in relation to fathers is similar in most major respects, and will not be presented here.

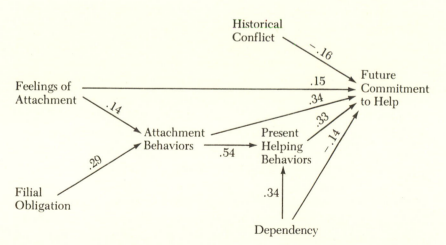

Figure 7-1 Path Diagram of Adult Children's Present and Future Help to Elderly Mothers.

Several salient features of the path diagram will be pointed out. First, attachment behaviors and dependency of the mother are the only variables to have a direct effect on the adult child's present helping behaviors. The effect of conflict was negligible, while the effects of both feelings of attachment and filial obligation on helping behaviors was indirect through their effects on attachment behaviors. All variables except filial obligation were found to have direct effects on future commitment to provide help, with the strongest effects noted for attachment behaviors and present helping behaviors. Attachment behaviors and dependency had an indirect effect on future commitment to help, acting through their effects on present helping behaviors. (Curiously, although the direct effect of dependency on future commitment is negative in sign, indicating an effect which lessens commitment to help, its indirect effect through helping behavior is positive.) Finally, both feelings of attachment and filial obligation have indirect effects on future commitment to help, acting through their effects on attachment behaviors.

Other Topics

Certain other topics which have not been taken up thus far are worthy of at least brief mention. First of all, the effects of widowhood on present helping behaviors and future commitment to help elderly parents have not been mentioned. It was found that whatever effect widowhood had on these variables was best represented by perceived parental dependency, since widowhood had no effect beyond that explained by dependency and dependency in itself had a stronger relationship. This seems reasonable when one considers the fact that many widows and widowers are not dependent and have no need for help from children. Where the elderly individual is perceived as dependent, widowhood is not the only factor involved.

Second, the effect of employment of middle-aged women on helping behavior to elderly parents and on commitment to provide future help has not been discussed thus far, although the entry of women into the work force has been proposed in the literature as a limitation on family support to the elderly. However, preliminary analyses indicated that women's employment status bore no significant relationship to helping behaviors or future commitment to help. Thus the hypothesis of the limiting effects of women's employment on family support can neither be supported nor rejected on the basis of the present data. In view of the fact that present help to elderly parents tended to be low for most adult children and future commitment tended to be only moderate, the failure to find a significant effect of employment status is not surprising. A small or moderate amount of help to elderly parents can be provided, job or no job, with only a small amount of strain to daily schedules and life style of the women involved. However, one can postulate a threshold effect here; when parental needs become great enough, the employed daughter can no longer accommodate the help required within her working schedule. Then, either help becomes limited or the job is jeopardized.

The final topic is concerned with adult children's responses to an open-ended question in the interview which asked, "At what point do you feel that you could no longer help your parents in their last years?" Some 29% of the study participants responded that there was no point at which their help to parents would diminish. Statements such as "I'd do whatever it takes," or "I'd take a leave from my job if necessary" were common. However, the remaining 71% listed a variety of situations in which their help would be limited or stopped, with 48% listing multiple situational factors. A strain in the adult child's marriage as a result of help to parents and a threat to the adult child's job were the most frequently reported of the situations, with negative effects on the adult children's own children the next most frequent factor. Less frequently reported were problems with the adult child's own health, mental and physical strains, and being unable to provide the type of health care required. Finances were considered to be a potential limitation on help by only 4% of adult children. The implication of these responses is that most adult children will go on helping their elderly parents as long as possible, limiting this help only if their marriage, their job, or their children's welfare were threatened by the extensiveness of the elderly parents' needs.

Summary

The present chapter was concerned with adult children's relationships with their elderly parents and how such relationships affected their provision of services to elderly parents.

The attachment behaviors of adult children (living close to parents and seeing or telephoning them frequently) were greater when parents were older, of lower socioeconomic status, and were perceived as more dependent with greater needs for services. By contrast, feelings of attachment (feelings of closeness, compatibility and values agreement with the parent and positive perception of the parent's traits) were not related to parental dependency. This fails to support previous studies which reported that adult children felt less close to dependent parents.

Feelings of attachment were related to attachment behaviors; those who felt closer also had greater contact with parents. The more conflict there was in the relationship, the less the feelings of attachment. This fails to support the view that strong positive and negative feelings tend to coexist.

Present provision of services to elderly mothers and fathers was greater, the more dependent the parent and the greater the attachment behaviors. Results of path analysis suggest that feelings of attachment and filial obligation have an indirect effect on present provision of services, acting through attachment behaviors.

The commitment to provide future services to parents was most strongly related to the adult child's attachment behaviors, with conflict, feelings of attachment, and dependency less strongly related. Path analysis indicated that filial obligation and feelings of attachment also had indirect effects on future commitment, acting through attachment behaviors; attachment behaviors and dependency had indirect effects on future commitment as well as direct effects. The commitment to provide services depended to some extent on traditional sex roles, with daughters feeling more commitment in traditionally feminine areas of service.

Personal strains experienced by adult children were directly related to the amount of services presently provided to elderly parents and to the perceived dependency of the parent. In relation to elderly fathers, where feelings of attachment were less, the personal strains associated with helping were greater. In regard to elderly mothers, children with a greater sense of filial obligation felt less strain. Daughters felt more strain than sons. Negative feelings toward fathers were greater, the greater the amount of services provided and the less the feelings of attachment. In regard to mothers, negative feelings were related to the perception of dependency, increased amounts of conflict, and less feelings of attachment and attachment behaviors.

The amount of services elderly parents received from adult children's siblings and other kin was greater, the greater the dependency and service needs of the parents. Expected future services from these family providers were related to greater feelings of family closeness. Clearly, the family helps when help is needed.

Future services from government agencies and voluntary organizations were expected to be greater by younger adult children with younger parents. This suggests a shift in attitudes toward these providers.

Future services from friends and neighbors were expected to be greater for younger, less dependent parents with fewer service needs. Friends and neighbors seem to be a more casual source of help, and are not expected to contribute much when needs for services become greater.

Hired future services were expected to be greater by those adult children with higher socioeconomic status who had less attachment behaviors and weaker feelings of attachment.

Chapter 8

VIEWS OF ADULT CHILDREN COMPARED WITH VIEWS OF THEIR ELDERLY PARENTS

Thus far, the adult children's views on their relationships with their elderly mothers and fathers and the help which they provide to their parents have been presented. The picture which emerges is that the adult children react in a positive way to providing services for their elderly parents when they perceive that such services are needed. However, from studying the adult children alone one cannot know how accurately they are judging their parents' needs for services or how effective and satisfactory the parents consider services provided by the adult children to be. The adult children may help their parents in areas in which the parents do not want or need help, or fail to give help in areas in which it is sorely needed. It is therefore very valuable to compare the views of adult children on the provision of services with those of their parents.

A recently completed study[1] of elderly citizens in the same midwestern city in which the current study was carried out provides a data base for making two types of comparison. The first type of comparison involves overall results of the first study of elderly adults compared with overall results of the present study of middle-aged adult children of elderly parents residing in the same community. The second type of comparison involves the responses of matched parent-child pairs from interviewees in the two studies. While the second type of comparison is the most sensitive way of detecting any differences in views, its value is limited by the fact that only 53 adult children whose parents were also interviewed were available for

149

study. Therefore, both types of comparison will be made. By looking at both, it may be possible to reach a conclusion about the degree of congruence between the views of elderly parents and their middle-aged adult children.

Comparison of Overall Results of Two Studies

In the earlier study,[1] 300 elderly residents of Lafayette, Indiana, who were over 60 years of age were identified by canvassing randomly selected blocks of the city. Fifty men and 50 women in each of the age ranges 60–69, 70–79, and over-80 were interviewed, making a total of 300 persons aged 60 to 94. All elderly persons who consented to participate in the study were interviewed individually in their homes except those who were too ill or who were judged to be senile.

Each interview lasted about two hours and elicited information on personal characteristics of the elderly and their kin, their relationship with various kin members, and their views on services. The elderly were asked about the amount of services which they now provided for themselves, and about the amount of help they now received from children and other kin, government agencies, voluntary organizations, friends and neighbors, and hired providers of services. They were also asked to indicate the importance of various services and the amount of help they desired from the various providers in time of future need.

The services investigated in the previous study of the elderly were the same sixteen services considered in the present study: homemaking, housing, home maintenance, income, personal care, home health care, transportation, social and recreation activities, psychological support, spiritual services, bureaucratic mediation, reading materials, employment, career education, enrichment education, and protective services.

The elderly persons interviewed in the study were primarily lower middle-class, Protestant, and Northern European in origin. Most study participants had some high school education, and most worked (or had worked) in skilled manual occupations and routine clerical or retail sales work. About half of the elderly persons interviewed were married and living with their husband or wife; 40% were widowed; and the remaining 10% were divorced, separated, or never married. Some 83% had at least one living child. Most of these elderly persons were relatively vigorous people who felt in control of their own lives. They had only moderate expectations for filial behaviors from their adult children.

One area of comparison between elderly and middle-aged adult children of elderly was the way the two generations viewed the importance of various kinds of services for the elderly. The elderly subjects were asked to rate the importance to them of each type of service on a five-point scale ranging from "very unimportant" to "very important." Mean scores for the elderly group were then arranged in order of their overall importance. Only twelve of the sixteen services were included in these ratings; homemaking, housing, maintenance, and income were not included because they were assumed to be of central importance to all. (The correctness of this assumption was borne out by the adult children's ranking of the importance of all sixteen services; these four services were ranked as highest in importance.) The middle-aged adult children of elderly were asked to rank all sixteen services according to the relative importance of the services to their parents, from "1" = "most important" to "16" = "least important." While the methods used for the elderly and middle-aged samples differ somewhat, an examination of the order of the mean ratings of the services by the elderly group and the mean rankings of the services by the middle-aged group provides a basis for a rough comparison of the views of the two generations.

Table 8-1 contains the twelve services rated by the elderly group arranged in order of their importance to, first, the elderly group and, second, the group of middle-aged adult children, with mean ratings presented for the elderly group and mean rankings presented for the middle-aged adult children.

The two groups agreed exactly on the relative ranks of four of the twelve types of services. Social and recreation activities were sixth in importance for both groups; spiritual services was eighth, employment services was eleventh, and career education was twelfth.

The elderly see their most important needs as involving protection, transportation, bureaucratic mediation, reading materials, and psychological support. The first three services were very close in mean ratings. In contrast, the adult children see their parents' most important needs as involving transportation, personal care, home health care, psychological support, and protection. Only three of these (transportation, psychological support, and protection) are found in the five most important services listed by the elderly, and

Table 8-1   Importance of Twelve Services to Elderly and to Middle-Aged Adult Children

Elderly Group			Middle-Aged Group		
	Rankings			Rankings	
Type of Service	Mean	SD	Type of Service	Mean	SD
1. Protection	4.14	1.12	1. Transportation	5.39	3.62
2. Transportation	4.09	1.22	2. Personal care	5.94	3.60
3. Bureaucratic mediation	4.03	1.22	3. Home health care	5.97	3.60
4. Reading materials	3.75	1.29	4. Psychological support	6.30	3.79
5. Psychological support	3.43	1.23	5. Protection	7.79	3.73
6. Social and recreation	3.23	1.35	6. Social and recreation	7.98	3.84
7. Enrichment	2.68	1.46	7. Bureaucratic mediation	8.12	3.83
8. Spiritual	2.55	1.40	8. Spiritual	8.58	3.66
9. Home health care	2.12	1.34	9. Reading materials	9.88	3.36
10. Personal care	2.11	1.38	10. Enrichment	11.80	3.56
11. Employment	1.70	1.42	11. Employment	13.87	3.25
12. Career education	1.66	1.08	12. Career education	14.20	2.59

of these three, protection was seen as most important by the elderly but only fifth in importance by the adult children. Bureaucratic mediation, viewed as third in importance by the elderly, was only seventh in the view of the adult children. Reading material, which was fourth in importance to the elderly, was only ninth in importance to the adult children. Finally, personal care and home health care were ranked as second and third in importance by adult children, but were seen as ninth and tenth in importance by the elderly.

Comparison of the responses of the two groups indicates that there are considerable differences between the older and the middle-aged generations on the relative importance of certain services. These differences may have practical consequences. If adult children disregard or even ridicule a service need which they see as unimportant while their parents see it as highly important, or if the adult children try to press a service upon parents who regard it as unimportant, the whole helping relationship may suffer. Parents, adult children, or both, may feel frustration and even anger when they feel the other does not appreciate their needs, views, or efforts.

Comparison of Views of Matched Parent-Child Pairs

There were 53 adult children interviewed in the present study who had a parent interviewed in the earlier study of the elderly. Of the 53 matched pairs, the elderly sample consisted of 23 men and 30 women, and the sample of adult children consisted of 26 men and 27 women. The mean age of the parents was 74.98 years and of the adult children was 46.96 years. The adult children were at slightly higher educational and occupational levels than were their parents. In these respects, this subsample was similar to the larger parent and adult child groups from which they were drawn.

To compare the responses of elderly parents and their adult children in regard to services presently provided by the children, matched-pair *t*-tests were carried out for each of 15 types of services and the total service score. (The two groups were not compared on employment services.) Table 8-2 contains means and standard deviation for parents and children and the *t*-values for the difference between groups.

Table 8-2   Differences in Group Means between Adult Children and Their Elderly Parents Regarding the Extent of Services Given by Adult Children at the Present Time

Type of Service	Elderly Parents		Adult Children			
	Mean	*SD*	*Mean*	*SD*	*t*	*p*
Homemaking	2.13	1.06	2.04	1.11	.63	.53
Housing	1.34	.90	1.43	1.20	−.68	.50
Income	1.30	.64	1.19	.56	1.14	.26
Home maintenance	2.36	1.05	2.28	1.36	.43	.67
Personal care	1.38	.86	1.30	.77	.73	.47
Home health care	1.34	.83	1.28	.79	.35	.73
Transportation	2.70	1.27	2.59	1.57	.64	.53
Psychological support	2.72	1.20	2.77	.90	−.29	.77
Social and recreation	2.87	.92	1.75	1.13	5.75	.00**
Spiritual	1.75	1.11	1.77	1.19	−.11	.91
Bureaucratic mediation	2.25	1.57	1.85	1.29	2.03	.04*
Reading materials	2.19	1.32	1.60	1.15	2.92	.01**
Career education	1.09	.35	1.02	.14	1.43	.16
Enrichment	1.30	.67	1.36	.68	−.42	.68
Protection	2.64	1.51	1.85	1.06	4.03	.00**
Total Service Scores	29.85	8.06	27.11	9.28	2.75	.01*

* Significant at the .05 level.
** Significant at the .01 level.

There were significant differences between the amount of services reported by elderly parents and by adult children for the total service score, and for the specific areas of social and recreation, bureaucratic mediation, reading materials, and protection services. Adult children in these cases reported providing fewer services than their parents reported receiving. This seems paradoxical, but since these services are regarded as quite important by parents, it may be that they regard their children's services in these areas as more significant than the adult children themselves do.

On the other hand, elderly parents and their children did not differ in reports of the amount of services provided in regard to homemaking, housing, income, home maintenance, personal care, home health care, transportation, psychological support, spiritual, career education, and enrichment services.

In the present study, adult children were asked to indicate the amount of service which they could provide to their parents at some future time when a great deal of help would be needed. Elderly parents were asked to indicate how much help they desired from their children in such a circumstance. Again, matched-pair *t*-tests were used to compare the responses of parents and their adult children. Results are presented in Table 8-3.

There was a significant difference in the overall future service score, with elderly parents desiring more services from children than their children felt committed to provide. This overall difference was borne out in significant differences in the specific service areas of home maintenance, social and recreational activities, bureaucratic mediation, reading materials, career education, and protection. Differences approached significance for transportation and psychological support.

There was no difference between the two groups in regard to homemaking, personal care, health care, spiritual, and enrichment services.

However, adult children felt a greater commitment to provide housing for their parents than the elderly parents desired. This is not surprising when one considers the strong desire of many older individuals to remain in their own homes at almost any cost.

Elderly parents were also asked how much help they desired to receive from various nonfamily providers in the future, while adult children were asked how much help they expected their parents to receive from such providers. Again, matched-pair *t*-tests were used to compare total scores for elderly parents and adult children in

Table 8-3 Differences in Group Means in the Extent of Future Services Desired by Elderly Parents and Adult Children's Commitment to Provide Such Services (N = 53)

Type of Service	Elderly Parents		Adult Children		t	p
	Mean	SD	Mean	SD		
Homemaking	3.58	1.40	3.62	.97	−.21	.84
Housing	2.83	1.75	3.49	1.27	−2.52	.02*
Income	2.74	1.64	3.04	.85	−1.26	.22
Home maintenance	3.69	1.30	3.25	1.07	1.99	.05*
Personal care	3.37	1.64	3.34	.86	.17	.87
Home health care	3.75	1.47	3.43	.95	1.51	.14
Transportation	4.09	1.38	3.70	1.38	1.75	.09
Psychological support	4.09	1.37	3.74	.63	1.78	.08
Social and recreation	4.34	1.07	2.94	1.03	7.87	.00**
Spiritual	3.50	1.60	3.24	1.29	1.06	.29
Bureaucratic mediation	3.98	1.47	3.40	1.17	2.41	.02*
Reading materials	4.08	1.25	3.40	1.08	3.29	.00**
Career education	2.18	1.45	1.53	1.03	2.69	.01**
Enrichment	2.76	1.47	2.40	1.32	1.17	.25
Protection	4.24	1.21	3.53	1.03	3.43	.00**
Total Service Scores	53.96	13.29	48.53	9.15	2.56	.01**

* Significant at the .05 level.
** Significant at the .01 level.

Table 8-4 Differences in Group Means in the Extent of Future Services Desired by Elderly Parents from Nonfamily Service Providers and Adult Children's Expectation of Such Services

Type of Service Providers	Elderly Parent		Adult Child		t	p
	Mean	SD	Mean	SD		
Government agencies	37.74	13.50	26.21	6.52	5.39	.00**
Voluntary organizations	38.53	12.23	25.66	6.44	6.66	.00**
Friends/neighbors	36.36	11.00	23.63	5.45	7.06	.00**
Hired help	29.08	7.28	23.11	5.84	5.52	.00**

** Significant at the .01 level.

regard to the different providers of services. The results are presented in Table 8-4.

In all cases, elderly parents desired more help than their adult children expected them to obtain from nonfamily providers—government agencies, voluntary organizations, friends and neighbors, and hired providers.

Table 8-5   Differences in Group Means between Elderly Parents and Adult
Children Regarding Closeness of Feeling, Value Consensus, and Filial
Expectation/Obligation

	Elderly Parent		Adult Child			
Variable	Mean	SD	Mean	SD	t	p
Closeness of feeling	3.87	.39	3.66	.55	2.84	.01**
Value consensus	3.04	.59	2.60	.79	3.13	.00**
Filial expectation/ obligation	17.19	3.12	18.96	2.81	−3.53	.00**

** Significant at the .01 level.

Comparisons were also made for certain measures of the parent-child relationship. In the study of elderly parents, measures were obtained for three of the variables used in the present study. These were closeness of feeling, value consensus, and filial expectation. (The adaptation of the filial expectancy scale used for adult children was termed "filial obligation.") Matched-pair *t*-tests were used to compare the responses of adult children and their elderly parents. The results are displayed in Table 8-5.

Elderly parents report greater closeness of feeling and value consensus with their adult children than the adult children report in regard to their parents. This asymmetry of feeling has been reported elsewhere in the gerontological literature as well.

However, the adult children reported feeling a greater sense of filial obligation than their elderly parents expected of them. This state of affairs was expressed by one of the middle-aged interviewees who stated, "I feel that I should do these things for my parents, but I don't expect my children to do them for me." Such a position would be understandable, but it seems inconsistent with the fact that the elderly desire more future services from their adult children than the children feel committed to provide. Certainly this sense of filial expectation on the part of elderly parents and filial obligation on the part of their children needs further study.

Summary

The views of adult children and their elderly parents in regard to services were compared using data from a recently completed study of the elderly carried out in the same community as the present study. From this data base, 53 parent-child pairs were identified.

Elderly parents and adult children differed somewhat in the relative importance that they attached to various services. Elderly parents saw protection, bureaucratic mediation, and reading materials as more important than did their children, while the adult children saw personal care and home health care as much more important than did their parents.

In regard to services provided by the adult children at the present time, elderly parents reported receiving more services from the children than the children reported giving. It may be that the parents regarded the children's services as more significant than the children themselves did.

In general, parents desired more services from their adult children in future time of need than their adult children felt committed to provide. These greater expectations extended to nonfamily providers as well, for elderly parents desired more future services from government agencies, voluntary organizations, friends and neighbors, and hired providers than their adult children expected them to obtain.

Elderly parents felt closer and felt greater value consensus with their adult children than the children felt toward them. However, adult children felt a greater sense of filial obligation toward their parents than their elderly parents expected of them.

Endnote

1. V. G. Cicirelli, "Social Services for Elderly in Relation to the Kin Network," Report to the NRTA-AARP Andrus Foundation (May, 1979).

Part Three

NEW DIRECTIONS

Chapter 9

SUMMARY OF THE STUDY

Recent studies in the literature and our own recently completed study for the Andrus Foundation[1] have found that most elderly people prefer to remain independent and take care of their own needs for as long as possible. This finding seems typical for the majority of elderly people who still live in the community, in contrast to the small minority (approximately 5%) who live in nursing homes or other institutions.

However, if people live long enough, sooner or later they must go through a period of deterioration or decline prior to death when they become more dependent on others for survival. For some, this period is short and ends abruptly; for others, it is a period of slow decline involving various chronic conditions that require long-term care.

When elderly people do feel that they need help, they prefer to receive it from their adult children above all others. As the world changes and contemporaries of the elderly die, their own children become more important to them as a mediating link to the outside world and as a source of affection.

Traditionally, adult children have been the primary support system for their elderly parents, and they continue to provide such help today. However, demographic, economic, and social trends in the modern world suggest that adult children may have to reduce the amount and kinds of help they can provide. If such is the case, the family support system must be evaluated for its limitations in meeting the needs of the elderly. Also, we must find out how it can be made more effective in the face of many present-day obstacles.

The present study was carried out to determine how adult children themselves view their role in helping their elderly parents.

Their views on helping are related to some of their own psychological characteristics and certain aspects of their relationship to their elderly parents.

The first set of research objectives of the study was to determine the adult children's perceptions of their elderly parents' needs for help, the adult children's present provision of help, their future commitment to provide help, their judgment of the relative importance of different kinds of help, the extent to which they experienced a burden while providing such help, and the amount of help to elderly parents from other providers.

A second set of research objectives was to determine certain perceptions, feelings, and behavior patterns characterizing the relationships of adult children to their elderly parents—perceived dependency of their elderly parents, feelings of attachment, filial maturity, conflict, and attachment behaviors.

A third set of research objectives was to determine relationships between the first two sets of variables; for example, between adult children's views on helping behavior and their perceptions, feelings, and behavior patterns toward their elderly parents.

Data were gathered in a field survey of 164 adults in a small midwestern city who had at least one living parent over 60 years of age. There were 75 men and 89 women in the sample; they ranged in age from 29 to 71. An interview questionnaire was administered at home by a trained interviewer to each adult who participated in the study. Questions probed personal characteristics of adult children and their parents, aspects of the parent-child relationship, and views on each of 16 types of helping behavior or services (homemaking, housing, income, maintenance, personal care, home health care, transportation, psychological support, social and recreation activities, employment, spiritual, bureaucratic mediation, reading materials, career education, enrichment, and protection).

Of the 164 middle-aged adult children of elderly, 89% were married and living with their spouse. The "average" interviewee was 46.3 years old and in relatively vigorous health. He or she had some college education or vocational training, and worked either in a clerical job, as a technician, or as a sales clerk. Some 91% of the men and 45% of the women worked full time. When both full- and part-time jobs were considered, 58% of all households interviewed had a woman in the work force. The "average" respondent had 2.81 children, with 1.48 still living at home. The subjects of the study had 81 living elderly fathers and 148 living elderly mothers; 80% of the fathers were still married, but 56% of the mothers were widowed. The average age of the parents was 74 years. They were at slightly lower educational and occupational levels than their children. Most of the elderly parents were retired and living in their own homes. Their overall health was seen as good by their adult children, in spite of a variety of health problems.

Views on Services to Parents

Both the adult children in the present study and their elderly parents in the earlier study[1] judged the various service areas in terms of their relative importance. The provision of housing, income, homemaking, and home maintenance services were seen as of central importance to everyone. Beyond this, adult children and elderly parents agreed that transportation was an important service, that psychological support and social and recreation services were moderately important, and that services to provide enrichment opportunities, spiritual and religious activities, and further career training and employment were unimportant. Most interesting were the areas of disagreement between adult children and their parents. Adult children considered services for protection, bureaucratic mediation, and obtaining reading materials relatively unimportant, while elderly parents considered them to be quite important. On the other hand, adult children considered home health care and personal care services to be very important, while elderly parents considered them to be relatively unimportant.

The great majority of adult children saw their elderly parents as having either very low needs or no needs for help from their children or other service providers. (This supports the findings of our earlier study that most elderly were relatively independent.) However, when adult children did perceive their elderly parents as having needs for services from others, they saw their parents as having the greatest needs at the present time in the areas of home maintenance, psychological support, transportation, bureaucratic mediation, homemaking, and protection services.

It is of interest that the areas in which adult children provided the most help to their parents were the same areas in which they saw their elderly parents as having the greatest needs: home maintenance, psychological support, transportation, bureaucratic mediation, homemaking, and protection.

Amounts of help provided to elderly parents were generally low, however. This was consonant both with the children's perceptions of low parental needs and with the earlier findings that elderly parents wanted to remain independent as long as possible.

Most adult children felt a considerable commitment to help their parents in a future situation where a great deal of help is needed. For most of the 16 service areas studied, only 12–15% of the adult children indicated *no* commitment to help in the future. At the other end of the scale, only a minority of adult children felt committed to providing all or almost all of their parents' needs. Thus, most adult children expected to provide only a moderate amount of help to their elderly parents in the future. Those giving more help now also felt a greater commitment to help in the future. Areas in which there was the greatest commitment to help were psychological support, housing, bureaucratic mediation, homemaking, and transportation services.

Certain relationships appear to exist between adult children's perceptions of the needs of elderly parents, their present help to parents, and their future commitment to provide help. The more adult children perceive their elderly parents as having needs for services in the present, the greater the amount of services they provide; this indicates their responsiveness to what they perceive as parental needs for help. Also, future commitment to provide a greater amount of help is related both to the adult children's perception of their elderly parents' needs and to their present provision of services. However, future commitment is more strongly related to present provision of services.

These relationships hold true for all services with the exception of home maintenance and housing. In the case of home maintenance, there is a relationship between perceived needs and present provision of services, but not to future commitment. As for housing, there is a future commitment, but little or no relationship to the present perception of needs or to provision of services. However, the relationships are weaker for such services as providing opportunities for enrichment, spiritual and religious activities, career training, employment, social and recreational activities, personal care, home health care, and provision of reading materials. These relationships are much stronger for homemaking, transportation, psychological support, protection, and bureaucratic mediation.

Overall, when adult children perceive their elderly parents' present needs for help, they respond to them. Furthermore, they feel a commitment to help their parents in the future. But, the degree of their present response and future commitment varies with the kind of help or service involved.

Stress associated with helping or caring behavior toward elderly parents was revealed in the personal strains and negative feelings experienced by adult children; these were low for most children. However, some degree of personal strains and negative feelings was found among a substantial proportion of the adult children interviewed.

Adult children did not view help from other providers as being very important to their parents. They reported their siblings as providing somewhat less help to parents now—and anticipated less in the future—than they themselves provided. Other kin were seen as occasional and supplementary service providers. The elderly parents' siblings and grandchildren were the kin members considered most likely to provide help now and in the future, while help from cousins, nieces, nephews, aunts, uncles, and so on was minimal or nonexistent. Nonfamily service providers (government agencies, voluntary organizations, friends, neighbors, and hired help) were viewed as having relatively limited and supplementary future usefulness as well.

Perceptions, Feelings, and Behavior Patterns

Most adult children perceived their elderly parents as only slightly to moderately dependent; this is congruent with seeing their parents as having low needs for services or help.

Most adult children reported relatively strong feelings of attachment to their parents. They felt close or extremely close to their parents and tended to agree about most values. There was a considerable feeling of compatibility in their relationships with parents, and most tended to view parents' traits quite positively.

Adult children felt only a moderate sense of filial responsibility toward their parents. Overall, there was not a great deal of conflict between adult children and their elderly parents, but most expected an increase in conflict if their parents were to live with them.

For 53 matched pairs of adult children and their parents (who were interviewed in the earlier study[1]), feelings of adult children were compared with the feelings of their own elderly parents. Elderly parents felt closer and reported greater values agreement with their children than their adult children did in return. On the other hand, adult children felt a greater sense of filial obligation to parents than their parents expected of them.

Adult children showed considerable attachment behaviors in their relationships with their elderly parents. The majority lived in the same city as their parents, and visited and telephoned them at least weekly.

Attachment behaviors of adult children were greater when parents were older, of lower socioeconomic status level, and were perceived as more dependent. By contrast, feelings of attachment were not related to parental dependency. Feelings of attachment were related to attachment behaviors; those who felt closer also had greater contact with parents. The more conflict there was in the relationship, the less the feelings of attachment.

How Perceptions, Feelings, and Behavior Patterns Affect Helping Behavior

The adult children's perception of the elderly parents' need for help is related both to the dependency of the elderly parent and to the adult children's attachment behaviors. Also, the older the parents, the older the adult child, and the less the education of the adult child, the greater are seen to be the needs of the elderly parents for various types of services. Daughters view their parents as having greater needs for help than do sons.

The adult children's present help to parents is most strongly related to the perceived dependency of the elderly parents and the adult child's attachment behaviors. Present help was greater, the older the adult child and the lower the educational level.

The commitment to provide future help to elderly parents is most strongly related to the adult children's present attachment behaviors; conflict, feelings of attachment, and dependency are less strongly related. The commitment to provide future services differed to some extent for sons and daughters, consonant with traditional sex roles (daughters for homemaking, sons for maintenance services, and so on).

Results of path analysis suggest that feelings of attachment and filial obligation have indirect effects, through their effects on attachment behaviors, on present provision of services and future commitment. Attachment behaviors and dependency had indirect as well as direct effects on future commitment.

The personal strains experienced by adult children were directly related to the amount of services presently provided to elderly parents and to the perceived dependency of the parents. The effect of other variables differed for the two parents. In regard to elderly fathers, personal strains were greater when feelings of attachment were less; in regard to elderly mothers, personal strains were greater for those with less sense of filial obligation. Daughters felt less strain than sons.

Predictors of negative feelings also differed for the two parents. Negative feelings toward fathers were greater, the greater the amount of services provided and the less the feelings of attachment. In regard to mothers, negative feelings were related to the perception of dependency, increased amounts of conflict, and fewer feelings of attachment and attachment behaviors.

The amount of present services which elderly parents received from the siblings of the adult children interviewed and from other kin was greater, the greater the dependency of the parents and the greater their consequent needs for services. Expected future services from these family providers were related to greater feelings of family closeness.

Future services from government agencies and voluntary organizations were expected to be greater by younger adult children, suggesting a shift in attitudes toward these providers. Friends and neighbors were viewed as a more casual source of help and were not expected to contribute much when need for services became greater in the future. Future services from hired providers were expected to be greater by adult children with higher socioeconomic status, fewer attachment behaviors, and weaker feelings of attachment.

Endnote

1. V. G. Cicirelli, "Social Services for Elderly in Relation to the Kin Network." Report to the NRTA-AARP Andrus Foundation (May, 1979).

Chapter 10

CONCLUSIONS AND IMPLICATIONS

Certain conclusions with both theoretical and practical implications can be drawn from the findings of the study. These topics will be taken up in this chapter.

Generational Differences in Views on Services

One of the findings of the study was that adult children and elderly parents have differing views regarding the importance or priority to be attached to various types of services to elderly. On the one hand, adult children do not seem to appreciate the concerns of elderly parents with crime and safety, or with the difficulties of dealing with the "red tape" of government agencies or businesses, or with a need to have sufficient reading material to maintain realistic contact with the world. On the other hand, adult children seem almost overly concerned about home health care and personal care in view of the relatively low priorities which the elderly attach to these areas.

Perhaps such differences in viewpoint reflect different values, a lack of sensitivity to elderly parents' needs, or problems in communication between parent and child. Adult children may still provide help to their parents even when they do not consider the parents' concerns as very important. However, in such cases the help may be insufficient or ineffective, or it may be given grudgingly, or the adult children may feel irritated or frustrated at "wasting time" on inconsequential kinds of help.

There is also the possibility that adult children may see needs, and urge acceptance of help, in areas which elderly parents do not see as

169

important. For example, a child may urge medical treatments which the parent does not wish to undergo. Not only present provision of services, but commitment to provide future services may be affected by these differences in priorities.

It is of interest to note that some of the more frequent conflicts between adult children and their parents are about things that the children feel the parents should do or about other aspects of the parents' activities. It is quite likely that many conflicts arise because of the two generations' different views on the importance of various types of help.

Attempts should be made to clarify and resolve such differences so that the viewpoints of each generation are more accurately understood and appreciated. By so doing, it may be possible to avoid a mismatch between what adult children provide and the kind of help that elderly parents desire. To achieve this end, discussion groups might be established—composed of adult children, elderly parents, or children and parents together—to exchange views, clarify values, and perhaps reach a consensus regarding the importance of various services. Such discussions could possibly provide a basis for more effective help to parents.

It is highly significant that adult children and elderly parents strongly agreed that further career training and employment services were unimportant. In fact, many adult children felt that career education and employment were notions almost too preposterous to consider in relation to their parents. However, there are decreasing government resources to maintain or increase Social Security and other benefits to the elderly, brought about by the inflationary economy and continuing demographic changes in the population structure, with increasing numbers of retirees to be supported by a decreasing proportion of workers. As a result of these pressures, proposals are now being considered to increase the age of eligibility for benefits to age 68. Mandatory retirement at age 65 has already been eliminated; at some later time a mandatory work age conceivably could be increased to age 70, or even 75. In such a climate, training for the elderly to maintain proficiency in their jobs, to shift to another type of occupation, or to reenter the job market will become much more desirable. As evidence mounts from psychologists and others that the older worker can perform proficiently and as this evidence is brought to general attention, career training and employment services will become more valued.

Some attempt to change these attitudes should be made, in view of the increasing numbers of elderly people in relatively good health and a less productive economy. Educational programs might be formulated specifically to educate both the elderly and their adult children on the capabilities of older persons, the possibilities for future work, and on the kinds of training which the elderly might undertake. Government agencies should work toward increasing realistic employment and career options for the elderly. In the present economic and political climate, this would seem to be a fruitful course for the government to pursue.

Myth and Countermyth

An important conclusion reached by many researchers in the past two decades is that the elderly have not been abandoned, isolated, rejected, or neglected by their adult children. The notion that such was the case has been labeled the myth of abandonment. Such a view was prevalent in the 1940s and 1950s, and has been largely dispelled by the accumulation of more recent research results.

However, in rejecting one myth, there may be a temptation to embrace an opposite conception, the countermyth that adult children automatically can and will provide adequate and effective help to their elderly parents. A recent study[1] has presented this sort of rosy outlook.

The results of the present study indicate that most adult children are providing relatively low amounts of services to their parents now and feel a commitment to provide only limited amounts of services to their parents in the future.

One might argue that adult children have a realistic assessment of their elderly parents' present situation as one in which there is a small degree of need for services from others. This argument could be supported further by the statements of the elderly parents who feel that they are taking care of most of their own needs at the present time and want to do so for as long as possible.

It is possible that elderly parents may need more help than they admit because they are reluctant to ask for help, feeling unwilling to give up their sense of independence or to burden their children. Subsequently, they do the best they can in providing for themselves, and their best may be less than adequate. Adult children, too, may be reluctant to make the effort to assess their parents' needs realistically.

If there is no problem at present, there may be a potential problem in the future. In our earlier study of the elderly,[2] one important finding was that elderly parents desired to receive help from their adult children above all other providers of services if they could no longer be independent. However, the adult children of the present study made it quite clear that they do not feel a commitment to provide for all, or even almost all, of their parents' needs in a future situation when needs become great. If elderly parents become sufficiently dependent, there may be conflict between the type and extent of help parents would like from their children and the help that adult children are willing to provide.

The present study suggested a phenomenon that we termed "filial anxiety." By this, we mean the experience of anxiety when anticipating the possibility of providing help to elderly parents. In the study, there seemed to be a stronger relationship of personal strains and negative feelings to perceived dependency of the parents than to actual provision of services. Indeed, some adult children reported strains when they were presently providing little or no help. The contemplation of such help in the future seems to induce anxious feelings in the present; it's as if the adult child were saying, "I have so many problems of my own to face. How can I take on such additional burdens? I'll go under if I do. Yet, I can see the first signs that such needs may lie ahead."

More studies are needed in order to know specifically the conditions under which adult children can and will provide effective help to elderly parents. Between the extremes of abandonment and total commitment are varying degrees of help to elderly parents.

Increasing Helping Behavior Through Attachment Theory

The attachment theory model of adult children's helping behavior to elderly parents as proposed in Chapter 2 received considerable support from the study. Perceived parental dependency and attachment behaviors were found to be strongly related to present helping behavior, and, in turn, present helping behavior and attachment behaviors were the strongest predictors of future commitment to help elderly parents. Feelings of attachment are directly related to attachment behaviors, but only indirectly related to helping behaviors and both directly and indirectly related to future commitment. Thus, adult children's attachment behaviors are much better predictors of present helping behaviors and future commitment to help than such other variables in the model as filial obligation or conflict.

Neither does filial obligation ensure helping behavior nor does conflict eliminate it.

The results suggest that appeals to a sense of duty in a direct attempt to stimulate adult children to help elderly parents may not be fruitful. It may be better instead to attempt to induce such attachment behaviors as visiting and telephoning, thereby promoting adequate and frequent communication between parent and child, as an indirect means of stimulating help to parents. (Appeals to duty might be expected to have more success if they were directed to attachment behaviors, rather than to helping behaviors per se.)

Since attachment behaviors were the strongest predictor of helping behavior and future commitment to help, then the communication processes between children and parents that are involved in attachment behaviors should be emphasized. An increase in the frequency of communication, though the bulk of the communication may consist of other matters, increases the likelihood that the adult child will learn of the elderly parent's problems and needs. Adult children should become more sensitive to the need for communication with elderly parents, and many of them need to be motivated to communicate more frequently and regularly. They need to take advantage of various modes and levels of communication, to supplement face-to-face visiting with telephoning, to supplement telephoning with letter writing if the child doesn't live near the parent, to consider tone of voice and nonverbal communication, and to "read between the lines" to determine the implications of what is said or left unsaid. If need be, the scope of communication should be enlarged so that parents and children can share feelings, worries, and concerns.

In short, adult children should be encouraged to communicate frequently with parents in order to become more aware of parents' needs and to respond to them. The inculcation of habitual patterns of communication is a desirable goal, as apparently the adult child's affection and duty are not sufficient bases for providing help to elderly parents. An existing pattern of attachment behaviors—that is, a well-established habit—is the best assurance that elderly parents will receive help from their adult children in the present and in the future.

A further means of improving adult children's helping behaviors is to help adult children become more knowledgeable about and aware of the aging process and the problems of the elderly, thereby increasing their sensitivity to their parents' needs.

Increasing Helping Behavior Through
Exchange Theory

From a theoretical standpoint, the study results substantiate the model of helping behavior presented in Chapter 2. On the other hand, some of the study results also are consonant with exchange theory. Stated simply, exchange theory holds that we maintain those relationships with individuals that maximize rewards and reduce costs. When applied to relationships between adult children and elderly parents, the relationship would be less rewarding and the costs higher as the parent becomes older and more dependent, increasing the imbalance in exchange of services.

Evidence for exchange theory from the present study comes from the adult children's limited future commitment at a time when the elderly parents are hypothesized to become older and more dependent, the filial anxiety at the anticipation of providing larger amounts of help in the future, and the existence of personal strains and negative feelings consequent to the provision of help. Thus, costs to the adult children become higher as parents' needs become greater. Although adult children's response is not reduced, future commitment to help is clearly much less than might be expected in the face of greatly increased parental needs.

From an exchange viewpoint, one might maintain adult children's motivation to provide help by providing incentives to do so (for example, tax rebates for helping family members), and by providing sufficient outside supports to reduce the degree of sacrifice required in order for the adult children to provide the needed services.

Socioeconomic Status

Socioeconomic status, as reflected in educational and occupational levels, was found to be a significant background factor that influenced adult children's relationships with their elderly parents. Adult children of lower socioeconomic levels showed greater attachment behaviors, saw their parents as having greater needs for services, and provided more help to their parents. Adult children at higher socioeconomic levels were more likely to be separated geographically, to have less frequent communication with their elderly parents, and to provide less help to them. In fact, adult children at higher status levels were more likely to favor using hired providers

of services for their parents. These findings support existing literature, and also indicate that socioeconomic status level must be taken
into account in evaluating adult children's provision of services to
parents. Lower-class or lower-middle-class adult children are more
concerned with direct provision of services to their elderly parents,
while upper-middle-class adult children are more likely to provide
money or hired help for the indirect provision of services.

The influence of socioeconomic status suggests the need to investigate more thoroughly the significance of such other background
variables as minority group status, relative ages of children and parents, and so on. The present study has contributed to the understanding of helping behaviors of adult children to elderly parents by
focusing on a population that has thus far been little studied: the
small midwestern city.

The Stress of Helping

The results of the present study indicated that some degree of personal strains and negative feelings is prevalent among a large proportion of the adult children of the elderly, and that the amount of
personal strains and negative feelings experienced by adult children
is related to the degree of dependency of elderly parents. Increased
personal strains are also associated with the amount of services provided to the parent by the adult child. Adult children who are older
report more personal strains and negative feelings; this is probably
due to the fact that older adult children also tend to have older,
more dependent parents and to provide more services to them than
younger adult children. Finally, women experience more personal
strains associated with helping behaviors than do men; this is supported by earlier findings that women play a major role in providing
services to the elderly.[3]

The personal strains that are most prevalent and which are most
strongly related to parental dependency seem to arise directly from
the helping relationship. They are not secondary problems with
spouse, children, finances, or job. Rather, the most crucial strains
involve a sense of physical and emotional fatigue and a persistent
feeling of being unable to satisfy the parent no matter what one
does. The adult child also experiences some loss of freedom associated with helping behavior, a feeling of being tied down by a
too-full daily schedule involving the parent, and having to curtail

certain social and recreational activities. The unpleasant emotions of impatience, frustration, and irritation are most strongly associated with having a dependent elderly parent, with feelings of guilt and helplessness entering the picture to a lesser degree.

Personal strains and negative feelings experienced by the adult child thus seem to be a natural accompaniment to the situation where an elderly parent becomes increasingly dependent and where increased helping behaviors are elicited. Such findings do not in themselves imply that the positive aspects of the relationship with parents are correspondingly diminished, although there are findings[4] that suggest that this may be the case.

Those adult children who provide the most help to their elderly parents are the ones who have the greatest stress. Such stress was revealed in the personal strains and negative feelings experienced by the adult children when helping their parents or providing care to them. However, when feelings of attachment to the parent are greater, there are fewer negative feelings. Greater feelings of closeness, greater compatibility, and more positive perceptions of the parents' traits all act to lessen negative feelings associated with helping dependent parents. Thus, the negative feelings are not only related to the provision of help to the parent, but are lessened when there are close feelings of attachment to the parent. By contrast, personal strains associated with helping behavior are not diminished by close feelings of attachment. Instead, such strains seem to be an inevitable accompaniment of the helping behavior itself, regardless of the closeness of the relationship to the parent.

The present study, then, emphasizes the importance of assessing negative side effects of providing services to elderly parents. If, for example, such negative side effects were to become too great, further helping behavior would be limited. Since elderly parents overwhelmingly prefer to receive help from their adult children when it is needed, and adult children seem willing to assume a reasonable burden of helping behavior, it is important to find practical means of minimizing resulting strains and negative feelings.

Minimizing the Burden of Care

One practical recommendation that has often been made is that government and social service agencies should provide supplementary or "back-up" services in areas which would be extremely burdensome for the adult child to handle alone. There has been much progress in this area. Certainly the scant evidence of financial hardship found in this study is testimony to the effectiveness of such programs as Social Security and Medicare, despite many current criticisms of these programs. More needs to be done in terms of making available supplementary part-time care or respite services. Services of this kind from the public or voluntary sectors may help to prevent an excessive buildup of personal strains and negative feelings which can culminate in family breakdown or parental abuse.

The psychologist or other professional can assume an important role in helping families with aging parents cope with their dependency needs. Counseling activities and self-help groups can provide an outlet where adult children can share their strains and feelings. Adult children can be helped to resolve conflicts and issues of earlier years which may influence their reactions to their parents, to gain a more mature perspective, and to learn to deal with dependent parents more effectively.[5-7]

To reduce stress on adult children, there are several possible approaches: provision of supplementary help (in which other kin or helpers from the community act to give the adult child relief from the burden of care) and opportunity for vacations or simple reduction of the daily load (as through day-care plans), for example. Government policy should help to provide for this kind of respite care, perhaps including pay for other kin who help. Group sessions, either self-help groups or groups with trained leaders, can provide a setting where adult children can share their problems and concerns and experience catharsis, develop skills for problem solving and coping, and provide mutual support. Where needs exist, more intensive counseling of adult children should be made available. Finally, home visits by other family members to provide emotional support to the adult child should be encouraged, since such visits have been found to ease the care givers' feelings of burden.

Adult Children: Focal Point of a Coordinated Service System

People who work with the elderly in any capacity are well aware of the need to find more effective means of coordinating services from various formal and informal providers. The results of the present study seem to imply that not only do adult children serve as primary care givers, but they may be the best coordinators of other service providers, especially as parents become older and more dependent.

Although adult children in the study were only partially committed to helping their elderly parents in the future, they do not expect any other provider to give more help than they themselves do. In effect, adult children may be depicted as not wanting to shoulder the entire burden of dependent parents' care, but not wanting to shift that burden to another provider, either. It is as if they want to maintain a central role in relation to their parents, but not be the only source of help. If so, the need to coordinate informal and formal providers is implied, but with adult children in a focal position in any such coordination.

Only adult children can truly individualize or tailor the care needed to fit the idiosyncratic situation and preferences of their elderly parents. Because of their special knowledge of the individuals concerned, adult children may be the best determiners of what type and degree of supplemental help or services should be provided. Help from other service providers can be increased as parents' needs become greater. (In family situations where there is little feeling of attachment, little attachment behavior, little sense of filial obligation, and much conflict, then it is likely that little help from adult children will be forthcoming and the role of providers should be increased.)

Although adult children may serve as the primary care givers and the best coordinators of other service providers, the importance of these other providers should not be downplayed. Federal aid is certainly important in regard to housing, Social Security, Medicare, and the like. Voluntary organizations such as the church may serve many purposes beyond spiritual needs. Hiring help, when money is available, allows elderly parents to maintain their independence and self-esteem. Obviously, many community agencies perform vital functions in serving the elderly.

Within the informal network, friends and neighbors can be depended on for various tasks—for example, checking up on daily well-being, transportation, minor errands—along with other family members. For example, when adult children of elderly parents are not available, they prefer help from siblings, nieces and nephews, and kin through marriage. (Kin through marriage are apparently a more important source of help than previously realized.)

Elderly parents seem to prefer different kin for particular kinds of help; for example, a daughter for homemaking, a son for help with government and business dealings, a grandchild for house mainte-nance, a sister for psychological support, and a cousin for spiritual help. With advancing age, the desire for help from these other kin increases, especially among the elderly over age 80. It is possible that the very old do not wish to burden their children exclusively.

The main point is that adult children can control, coordinate, and monitor the quality of care giving from not only formal providers but from within the kin network itself. They may be in a better position to communicate and solicit supplementary help from other kin, especially if the elderly parents are ill or senile or reluctant to ask family members for help.

If adult children are assumed to have such a crucial role, and if there is more than one adult child in the family, it is important to consider the relationships between adult children and their siblings when helping elderly parents. Sibling rivalry may still exist in adult-hood, either in latent or active form, and may interfere with effective helping behavior toward elderly parents. There may be rivalry when siblings must coordinate their activities to help ailing parents. One adult child may complain that the other is trying to take over and "boss" everyone, or that the other is not doing his or her share, or that the parents have always liked one sibling better than the others, and so on. Such feelings may disrupt any cooperative endeavor between siblings and reduce the amount of help provided to elderly parents. For example, one sibling might say, "Mother always liked Susie better than me. Let Susie take care of her now."

Siblings must learn to overcome their rivalries and develop cooperative behavior in order to reach a consensus as to how best to help elderly parents. Fortunately, the research indicates that as adult children become older, they do mellow in regard to their rivalries and tend to become more cooperative.[8]

Endnotes

1. S. E. Rix and T. Romashko, *With a Little Help from My Friends* (Washington, D. C.: American Institute for Research, 1980).
2. V. G. Cicirelli, "Social Services for Elderly in Relation to the Kin Network," Report to the NRTA-AARP Andrus Foundation (1979).
3. L. E. Troll, "The Family of Later Life: A Decade Review," *Journal of Marriage and the Family*, 33 (1971), pp. 263–290.
4. B. N. Adams, *Kinship in an Urban Setting* (Chicago, Ill.: Markham Publishing Company, 1968).

5. W. H. Quinn and G. A. Hughston, "The Family as a Natural Support System for the Aged." Paper presented at the 32nd Annual Scientific Meeting of the Gerontological Society, Washington, D.C. (1979).
6. L. Troll, S. J. Miller, and R. C. Atchley, *Families in Later Life* (Belmont, Calif.: Wadsworth Publishing Company, 1979).
7. I. E. Hudlis, "A Group Program for Families of the Aging: A Service Strategy for Strengthening Natural Supports." Paper presented at the 30th Annual Scientific Meeting, Gerontological Society, San Francisco, California (November, 1977).
8. V. G. Cicirelli, "Sibling Relationships in Adulthood: A Life Span Perspective," in L. W. Poon (Ed.), *Aging in the 1980s* (Washington, D.C.: American Psychological Association, 1980), pp. 455–462.

Chapter 11

PARENT CARING: A LIFE SPAN PERSPECTIVE

The present chapter goes beyond the findings and conclusions of the present study. It is admittedly more speculative in nature; yet it represents further implications from the results of the study.

A Life Span Perspective

The present study was concerned with the helping of elderly parents by adult children. However, when such help is conceptualized within a life span perspective, it takes on a new meaning. From a life span perspective, one can appreciate and come to understand the intricate relationship between child rearing and parent caring. During the early part of the life span, parents provide food, clothing, shelter, love, and guidance for the child. These things are essential for the child's survival, development, and eventual independence in young adulthood.

During child rearing, there is an imbalance in the exchange of help in favor of the child. If parents care sufficiently for the child, they will meet whatever obstacles occur and make whatever sacrifices are needed to carry out the responsibilities of child rearing. Through all this, the child develops the basic attachment bond that provides a foundation for all later relationships. At this stage of life, one also finds filial idealization, where children tend to perceive their parents as more idealized beings than they do at any other stage of life.

When the child is in young adulthood and the parent is in middle

181

age, there is more balance in the exchange of help. Middle-aged parents may baby-sit with grandchildren, help with finances, and so on, while the young adult may assist the parent with house maintenance, occasional transportation, and the like. There is greater mutual exchange of help (but not necessarily an equal exchange), as well as relative independence of child and parent from each other. Filial idealization leads to filial disenchantment.

In the later part of the parents' life span, when the child has grown to middle age, the exchange of help may shift more in favor of the elderly parent. The process has become reversed. Child rearing was essential for the survival, maintenance, development, and eventual independence of the child. At this stage of life, parent caring is essential for the maintenance and continued survival of the elderly parents in view of their decreasing growth and increasing dependence. Middle-aged adult children must now care enough and make sufficient sacrifices to help their elderly parents. Filial disenchantment gives was to filial maturity.

If one conceives this sequential shift in the exchange of helping behavior throughout the life span as a necessity both for species survival of the young and fulfillment of the elderly's potential life span before death, then parent caring and child rearing become intrinsically related. Keeping these aspects of mutual help in a finely tuned balance over the life span would then seem to be an end in itself for the species, although the degree to which such an end has been attained has varied throughout the centuries, depending upon the social forces at various times. Unfortunately, the social forces operating today may disrupt the child rearing and parent caring mechanism more than in any previous decade or century.

Among all the forces mentioned earlier in this book, two stand out as unique to our time. These require further elaboration. First, in the earlier decades of this century, most elderly parents died while in their sixties or seventies. Now, an ever-increasing number are living into their eighties or nineties. This adds to parent caring, since more of these very elderly parents have chronic health conditions and are very dependent, requiring care over a greater time period then before. (Parent caring, even under these conditions, helps the parent fulfill the full potential of the life span. Of course, the ideal is to increase both the length and the quality of life.) Second, divergent family forms (divorce, remarriage, single-parent household, gay marriage, "living together," communes, and so on) have greatly increased throughout the society and will probably continue to do so into the foreseeable future.

Without placing any moral judgment on any of these alternative family forms, they may have the consequence of disrupting the helping relationships between adult children and elderly parents. In the traditional family form, which may become a minority type in the future, the family was considered as a lifetime arrangement. Consequently, there was a stronger commitment to family members. The divergent family forms do not seem to produce this degree of commitment, since individuals can easily obtain divorces or move in and out of a relationship that requires no legal binding or other formal commitment.

The net effect of such forces may be a dramatic disruption of the child rearing and parent caring system throughout the life span. The unwillingness or lack of commitment of adult children to help their elderly parents to the extent that previous generations did may be related to increased filial anxiety rather than filial maturity. In other words, filial anxiety may become the dominant theme of the middle-aged children rather than filial maturity. These are not mutually exclusive concepts, but perceiving one's parents as persons in their own right may be secondary to the anxious feelings one might have in anticipating the care of that parent.

Although the elderly are living longer, filial anxiety and reduced commitment to provide help on the part of adult children may nevertheless prevent them from attaining the full potential of their life span or from maximizing the quality of their life. This statement becomes even more true if Brody[1] is correct in stating that the advanced elderly have no place to go but to institutions or to live with children.

Inflation is rapidly placing the cost of institutions out of financial reach for the average family. If, therefore, large numbers of elderly parents go to live with their middle-aged children, there is no certainty that such living arrangements will be a satisfactory solution for many parents.

The same adult children who have entered into divergent family forms may provide inadequate child rearing to their own young children, thus reducing the survival rate of the young or failing to provide for adequate development. The increase in child abuse in recent years is one aspect of this picture. Young children, in turn, may continue the cycle by providing less parent caring in their adult years.

In short, it is hypothesized that parent caring is part of an intergenerational life span sequence reciprocally related to child rearing. Both child rearing and parent caring can have influences on each other, for better or worse, for more than one individual, and, by implication, for a society or, ultimately, for the species. If one perceives parent caring in this way, one must evaluate it from a life span perspective, assessing the quality of both child rearing and parent caring and their relationship to each other within a culture or subculture.

Help with Helping

With respect to parent caring, there are many programs evolving today whose stated goals are to help the adult children maintain their physical and mental health while simultaneously learning how to deal with and help elderly parents more effectively.

Such programs may emphasize instruction, or education, or training in skills; or they may be therapeutic in nature (concerned with handling feelings and emotions); or some combination of these. They may use individual or group approaches, or a combination of the two.[2-5]

Instructional programs provide information about age-related changes in physical, mental, emotional, and social functioning. They also consider common problems of the elderly, such as finances, living arrangements, health, widowhood, loss of friends and kin, and common emotional reactions. Adult children can then know better what to expect as parents grow older. They can judge what is normal and expected, and not be misled by myths and stereotypes about old age.

Information is also provided about community resources available to the elderly and to adult children, and how to make use of these resources. Some programs also consider the typical changes and problems of middle-aged adults. Adult children, through increased self-knowledge and self-understanding, may be able to deal more effectively with problems arising during parent care.

Programs concerned with skill training attempt to teach adult children to recognize the symptoms, deal with the feelings, and manage the behavior of the elderly in order to facilitate their direct dealings with their parents. For example, they might learn how to communicate with parents who are losing hearing or vision, or how to care for a parent who has paralysis from strokes, chronic depression, or Alzheimer's disease. They might learn general interpersonal skills, such as listening carefully, showing acceptance, making decisions, and solving problems. These skills will help the adult children to cope with the many diverse problems that arise in caring for elderly parents.

Another aspect of skill training would help the adult children to deal with personal problems that may reduce their effectiveness. For example, they may need to learn how to pace themselves, or to develop strategies to dissipate or prevent stress.

Programs which are therapeutic in nature aim to reduce stress or burden on the adult child, provide emotional catharsis, give emotional support, and maintain morale. For example, through group sessions which allow adult children to express feelings of frustration in dealing with parents, to realize they are not unique in having such problems, and to experience the camaraderie of others with similar problems, the adult children may experience relief and emotional support. Adult children may share common problems and concerns, consider various options together, learn to resolve specific conflicts with parents, become aware of the range of emotions which they feel in connection with the parent relationship, and learn to modify or accept their situation.

Most of the programs that currently exist are limited in their comprehensiveness. Very few have attempted any kind of evaluation for their effectiveness. However, there is a clear need for such programs, whether formal or informal, and certainly they should be encouraged.

The Process of Helping

The study reported in this book was concerned with various factors related to adult children's helping behaviors and future commitment to help their elderly parents. A further concern should be with a more detailed model of the helping process, involving the various psychological steps which occur en route to effective helping behavior. A cognitive awareness of the psychological steps in helping can enable the adult child to gain both insight and control over the process, regardless of how much information, skill training, or emotional therapy is available.

There are six general steps in the process of helping. They are:

1. Considering the prerequisites for helping
2. Diagnosing the need for help

3. Making the decisions to help
4. Implementing the decisions
5. Determining the effectiveness of help
6. Revising helping behavior

Prerequisites for Helping

There are two vital ingredients necessary for parent caring to be effective: the adult child's sustained motivation, and the capability to help. The adult child must perceive a reason to be involved in helping and to maintain helping behavior over a period of time. As discussed in earlier chapters, feelings of attachment, attachment behaviors, filial obligation, conflict with parents, and previous helping behaviors are all factors involved in motivating an adult child's helping behavior.

The adult child must assess his or her expertise, physical and mental health, financial resources, available time, and other commitments to determine whether there is a basis for helping behavior. If the motivation to help is sufficiently strong, the adult child may reestablish priorities, obtain special training or support, or make changes in his or her life style in order to increase the capability to help the parents. However, if there is neither the motivation nor the capability to help, there is little likelihood that any effective help will flow from child to parent.

Diagnosing the Need

Diagnosing the elderly parents' needs for help involves first detecting that some kind of need exists and then assessing just what the need is. Many adult children lack sensitivity regarding the needs of their parents, or they are so involved with their own lives that they are simply unaware of the parents' needs, or they are so utterly selfish that they deliberately ignore their parents' concerns. Another possibility is that they may value the importance of various services differently than their parents do, and therefore not be concerned about their parents' needs in certain areas until real difficulties develop. However, by asking the question "Are my parents able to take care of their needs in various areas?" and trying to become more alert to signs that they are not, adult children can become more sensitive to their parents' needs and concerns as they interact with them.

Once there is an awareness that a need exists, adult children must learn to recognize symptoms and to understand the meanings behind certain parental behaviors in order to make an adequate assessment of what is wrong and what is needed. Adult children sometimes exaggerate the signs of aging, jump to conclusions regarding parents' complaints, identify any parental expression of feelings as a serious problem, ignore psychosocial and ego needs. A hasty or inadequate diagnosis (or misdiagnosis) can lead to faulty decisions regarding help. For example, a parent may need some help during a recovery period following a heart attack before he is able to function independently again. A child, viewing the condition of the parent soon after the attack, may conclude that the parent needs permanent nursing home placement. By allowing time for a more complete diagnosis of the needs, such a drastic change in living arrangements could be avoided.

Adult children may easily misdiagnose physical complaints or symptoms. Some children label the first sign of forgetting as senility; some label errors caused by poor hearing as mental confusion; some may interpret a parent's first signs of physical slowing as an indication that the parent should give up participation in many activities; some may interpret a parent's complaints as a sign of depression when a parent may simply want someone to share feelings and show caring.

Adult children may be insensitive, ignorant, or denying of their parents' ego needs, sexual needs, achievement needs, needs for physical attractiveness, needs to feel important, needs for change (or needs for stability), and so on. On the other hand, adult children may diagnose their parents' needs in a realistic manner, only to have the elderly deny them. Or both parents and children may concur in a misdiagnosis.

Informational programs may be of considerable value in helping to make a realistic assessment of the needs of elderly parents. This is a key first step in the helping process.

Decisions about Helping

Once their parents' needs for help have been diagnosed, adult children must reach a decision as to whether or not they will give some sort of help in the situation. Considering their motivation to help and their capabilities, the adult children might consider the consequences of helping to themselves, to the elderly parents, and to significant others. Such questions as the following might be asked: Do I have sufficient resources? Do I want to help with this need, no matter what? Will the burden or the cost be too great? Do my parents expect too much help? Will helping bother their pride or damage their sense of independence? At some point, the adult children make a decision to help or not to help.

Once the first decision has been made, the second decision is to determine what kind of help should be given. It may be difficult to find the kind of solution which would be most effective to meet a particular need. Again, informational programs may be useful in suggesting a variety of options to consider. For example, if a parent wishes to give up a large home, should the new home be with a child, in an apartment, a retirement village, a smaller home in the suburbs, a nursing home, a communal living group, or some other arrangement? Who should help is a second concern. Should the adult child help the parent directly? or hire someone to help? or solicit help from a public agency? Often, there is one adult child among the adult children of the family who is especially well qualified to give a particular type of help.

When to help is still another part of the helping decision: the timing can be important. Delaying help for too long can allow a formerly manageable situation to develop into a crisis. On the other hand, parents may complain and seem to require much help, but if the situation is analyzed closely, it will become clear that helping may encourage them to become overly dependent at a time when they are still able to do for themselves. In our culture, self-sufficiency and independence are valued highly and are closely associated with the individual's self-esteem. In some cases, the best thing to do may be to encourage the parents to remain self-sufficient for a while longer, or to join with elderly friends in a self-help program.

A question closely allied to the timing of help is that of how much help should be given. Adult children must keep from providing too much help, when that help may rob elderly parents of independence or allow the children to dominate their parents. On the other hand, even when the need for a great deal of help is clear, adult children must determine how much help they can give before it disrupts their own lives. Total sacrifice to help parents will be self-defeating if it leads to a breakdown of the child or the child's family. Also, it makes a difference if the help is to be given for a few days during a crisis or is to be a long-term arrangement. To answer "How much help?" must involve consideration of both the needs of the elderly and of the adult children.

Implementing the Decisions to Help

When adult children have reached decisions about whether to help, what kind of help, how much help, and when it should be given, the decisions need to be implemented. Seemingly, this should be a simple matter, but it is often not as simple as it appears. Adult children may need to negotiate the provision of help with elderly parents. Parents may not like to ask for help or to accept it because of pride; there is an implication that one has less power and is subservient to another. Adult children may not like to offer help to parents directly for fear of insulting them.

Parents and children need to develop effective means for communicating about needed help. Parents may exaggerate complaints or act martyred to arouse guilt in the adult children without actually asking for help. Or, parents may simply get angry if children don't fulfill their needs without being asked. Some parents never ask for help; they demand it, thereby producing negative responses in the children. Parents often feel reluctant or unable to discuss their needs and desires in regard to help with their children. They don't want to feel like a "case" or a patient about whom something should be done. If they value independence, they don't want their adult children telling them what kind of help they should have, how, and when. On the other hand, adult children may need to schedule their helping activities in order to manage all their responsibilities. Children may feel frustrated if parents don't accept their solutions to problems. One could go on and on with examples of this type.

Adult children may not know how to help, or how to help in the right way, while elderly parents may not know how to solicit help or to accept it. These problems become especially difficult when the parents' ego and psycho-social needs are involved. Programs which stress skills in the helping situation may be valuable to adult children who are having problems in this area.

Additional problems can arise in the process of providing help. Efforts of more than one provider (other family members and non-family providers) may need to be coordinated and areas of responsibility delineated in order to maintain harmonious relationships with other helpers. Siblings may develop resentments if one feels that another is not doing enough. Also, side effects of helping on the adult children must be dealt with. Some personal strains and negative feelings are probably inevitable, as human relationships all have negative as well as positive aspects. If such side effects are greater than anticipated or are too stressful, helping behavior may ultimately be reduced.

Determining Effectiveness of Helping Behavior

Once a planned type of help has been given, or is in process, adult children must assess the effectiveness of the help being provided. There is little evidence in the literature about how effective adult children are in satisfying their parents' needs. If, for example, the adult children are shopping for the parents, are they able to get the things the parents want at the expected price and within a suitable time? How well does the help meet the parents' needs? Is it emotionally satisfying to the parents? What are the effects on the children providing the help and on their families? If a particular course of home health treatments is being given, is it having a positive effect?

Revising Helping Behavior

If the results of helping behaviors are not meeting the need or are not satisfying to elderly parents, or have negative side effects on the adult children, then the children must be flexible enough to revise their help accordingly. Otherwise, adult children may be providing help which is useless or which is nothing more than well-meaning interference into the lives of their parents. Adult children may be able to discuss the problem with their parents and arrive at a more effective means of helping. Or children may seek help from a group program, in order to learn helping skills or new options.

In sum, the interaction between adult children and their parents in the process of helping is not a simple matter. If adult children have the motivation and capability to help their parents, they must then be able to diagnose accurately the needs for help, make appropriate decisions about providing help. They must implement the helping decision through negotiating with the parents and then acting, and then determine the effectiveness of the help and modify the helping behavior accordingly. If such a model helps to direct the helping process by making its steps more explicit, then it may prove useful in various training programs.

Obligations of Elderly Parents

Adult children's helping behavior to parents may be reduced or made more difficult by the gap between generations and by parental characteristics. Just as between parents and adolescents, there is a gap between middle-aged children and their elderly parents. The size of the gap changes with each decade, depending on the rapidity of changes occurring in the culture and the nature of such changes. The difference in background, experiences, and life styles for each generation makes it difficult at times for adult children to understand and appreciate the needs of their elderly parents. The converse may also be true, for elderly parents may not understand and appreciate the needs and problems of their adult children.

Although the elderly have been through the stage of mid-life, it was at a different time. Also, people tend to become more egocentric with increasing age, seeing the world exclusively from their own perspective. Elderly parents may take it for granted that everyone should live the way they do. Finally, after not living closely with their children for many years, they may not appreciate the degree of change in life style that has taken place in their children.

Parents may also have difficult personality characteristics. We now tend to glorify the elderly, as we did the youth in our culture in the 1960s. To some extent this represents a needed change from the negative stereotyping of the aged which has been so prevalent in the past. However, there are many elderly people who are demanding tyrants to their children (and to others), who pretend helplessness, who are unduly rigid, or who delight in being impossible to deal with.

Perhaps elderly parents should be brought together to learn about the developmental changes of middle age and the problems that adult children face in today's world, to learn how to appreciate the efforts of adult children, and to learn how to cooperate with them, especially if they desire help from adult children. Perhaps elderly parents *can* change in various ways to make the provision of help to them easier for their adult children. Perhaps they can learn to be more flexible and to fit into the times. Compromise with the younger generation may be more meaningful and satisfying to both generations than a totally egocentric position or a pretense of great wisdom.

New Role for Adult Children

As we have often reiterated in this volume, most elderly people want to be self-sufficient and independent for as long as possible. But this fundamental need may not have been given sufficient attention in programs planned to help the elderly.

Perhaps adult children should adopt a more preventive approach to their elderly parents' needs by helping their parents to find ways of learning and growing to meet their own needs both before and during the period of decline. By so doing they may in the long run be forestalling decline. Adult children at present place too much emphasis on "support" strategies of helping in which they try to provide whatever the elderly parents need.[6] This may lead to learned helplessness and dependency, while training and motivational strategies may be more efficacious in prolonging independence and self-sufficiency.

Adult children can be a constant source of emotional support and inspiration to parents, encouraging them to have hopes, dreams, ambitions, new goals, and new horizons. Adult children can help their parents to stay involved with life, to ignore negative stereotypes about aging, and to take new risks. As do parents who are there to provide a "backup" to adolescents reaching out for new experiences, so can adult children provide the same support while elderly parents try new things: travel, a love affair, or a new occupation.

Adult children can help their parents to help themselves as much as possible and for as long as possible, rather than allowing them to depend unnecessarily on family or society. Adult children can provide the resources and support to promote parents' self-care and self-help, rather than emphasize direct services. For example, if adult parents need transportation, cannot adult children encourage and help them to improve their driving skills rather than chauffeuring them everywhere? If elderly parents need a change of scene, cannot adult children help them to plan an excursion or vacation and encourage them to try it on their own, rather than taking them? If elderly parents need love, a friend, or a sex partner, cannot adult children counsel them to take a risk on a new relationship, regardless of age?

Most people agree that the goal of life is to live as fully as possible until near death rather than to decline slowly for years, and there is new evidence that this is possible.[7] Perhaps, through self-help, elderly parents can maintain a fuller life for a longer period of time than if they depend prematurely on family and society. If this is the case, adult children could help best by playing a more supportive role in encouraging elderly parents to attain a self-helping life style. Such an approach could pay unexpected dividends for adult children in later years through the changed attitudes with which they confront their own aging.

Endnotes

1. S. Brody, "What Will We Do About Gramps," *The Miami Herald* (March 30, 1981), p. 1C.
2. M. E. Hartford and R. Parsons, "Uses of Groups with Relatives of Dependent Older Adults." Paper presented at the 32nd Annual Scientific Meeting of the Gerontological Society, Washington, D.C. (1979).
3. I. E. Hudlis, "A Group Program for Families of the Aging: A Service Strategy for Strengthening Natural Supports." Paper presented at the 30th Annual Scientific Meeting, Gerontological Society, San Francisco, California (November, 1977).
4. W. H. Quinn and G. A. Hughston, "The Family as a Natural Support System for the Aged." Paper presented at the 32nd Annual Scientific Meeting of the Gerontological Society, Washington, D.C. (1979).
5. A. G. Silverman, C. I. Brahce, and C. Zielinski, *As Parents Grow Older* (Ann Arbor, Mich.: Institute of Gerontology, 1981).
6. J. Karuza and I. J. Firestone, "Cross-Generational Helping: Preference for Alternative Helping Strategies." Paper presented at the 33rd Annual Scientific Meeting of the Gerontological Society, San Diego, California (November, 1980).
7. J. F. Fries, "Aging, Natural Death, and the Compression of Morbidity," *The New England Journal of Medicine* (July 17, 1980). pp. 130–135.

INDEX